Ainsley de Jong Could Dance

Aaron de Jong
and Peter Doherty

Ainsley de Jong Could Dance

Published in 2023 by Heads & Tales an imprint of Hardie Grant Media

Hardie Grant Media (Melbourne)
Level 1, Building 1, 658 Church Street
Richmond VIC 3121, Australia

www.hardiegrant.com.au

A catalogue record of this book is available from the National Library of Australia.

A catalogue record for this book is available from the National Library of Australia

Ainsley de Jong Could Dance
ISBN 9780646879499

Publication commissioned by Courtney Nicholls
Publication managed by Hannah Louey
Edited by Joanne Holliman
Cover design by George Saad
Typeset in 12/17pt Adobe Garamond Pro by Cannon Typesetting
Printed in Australia by Opus Group Pty Ltd, an Accredited ISO AS/NZS 14001 Environmental Management System printer.

The paper this book is printed on is certified against the Forest Stewardship Council® Standards. Griffin Press – a member of the Opus Group holds chain of custody certification SCS-COC-001185. FSC® promotes environmentally responsible, socially beneficial and economically viable management of the world's forests.

... tenderness is the art of personifying, of sharing feelings, and thus endlessly discovering similarities. Creating stories means constantly bringing things to life, giving an existence to all the tiny pieces of the world that are represented by human experiences, the situations people have endured, and their memories. Tenderness personalizes everything to which it relates, making it possible to give it a voice, to give it the space and the time to come into existence, and to be expressed.

Olga Tokarczuk, The Tender Narrator, Nobel Lecture
The Nobel Prize in Literature 2018, 7 December 2019

Contents

PART 1

From 'The Stolen Child'

Come away, O human child!
To the waters and the wild
With a faery, hand in hand,
For the world's more full of weeping than you can understand.

W.B. Yeats, 1889

CHAPTER 1

She was pretty special

AINSLEY DE JONG could dance.

She could dance, she could sing, she could laugh.

She could make *you* laugh, this little girl with the face of a cherub. A sweet, smiling face fronting a fierce independence, with a knack for comedy and joy beyond her years that was more than enough to draw people in.

'When Ainsley was the centre of attention, she loved it,' her mum Amanda says. 'And if she wasn't, she could make sure she was. She loved the stage. Even at the end-of-year school dances, "Ains" just ran the show. She laughed – a lot! – and was very much happy to be front and centre. She was also very stubborn, too, in some ways.'

Ainsley de Jong brought people in tight with her engaging personality and trademark resilience. From there, right up close, anyone could see what she was made of: character and courage. In equal parts.

Truth be told, those all-dancing, all-singing performances weren't for Ainsley. They were from her. A gift offered up by a little girl who, left to herself, would've been just as happy on her own in another room.

'If there was a heap of kids around, it'd be too busy for her,' Ainsley's dad Aaron says. 'She'd back up into the corner, quietly work her way around and go to be by herself in the other room. But if you said, "Ains, show us a dance", she'd just turn around and come and put on a show for you.'

~

You can imagine the pride in Ainsley's parents. It runs rich in their voices; it is written in their faces, glowing with delight at the memories of a remarkable daughter who became something of a celebrity for the way she took on cancer.

'At the hospital in Wagga, and in Sydney, nurses would see her coming and yell her name out down the hallway,' Aaron says. 'She put everyone in a good mood.'

This little girl, who could wow the crowd at a Christmas concert or a family gathering, had honed her act in hospital wards, refining her performances of comedy and kindness through years of doctors' appointments and chemotherapy treatments. She overcame a marathon brain tumour operation as an infant, defying the odds for more than seven years to keep the cancer at bay.

'She'd have the nurses and medical staff all in stitches. And then she'd thank them with her little "thank you",' Amanda says, mimicking the sweet little voice that belied a big, fighting spirit. That she would see Ainsley advance to the point of being up on stage at a school concert still blows Amanda away.

'I don't think I've ever felt as proud,' she says. 'She was pretty special. We used to watch her and think, "Oh my God! She's been through so much." We'd all been through it together. We'd think back to all the treatments, even down to the occupational therapy and stuff where she just used to *scream*. I'd think, "*That's* what got you up on the stage." Ha!'

Going to school, performing on stage, being a big sister: they were all big goals for Ainsley. Goals she achieved, things she was excelling at. They were unimaginable ideas for much of her early life after a brain tumour was discovered when she was almost four months old. Survival, then, was Ainsley's only concern. And that's how it was going to be for some time to come. But Aaron and Amanda's daughter was already plotting a course in doing her parents proud.

'Every three months, she would have an MRI in Sydney,' Aaron recalls of Ainsley's treatment under the care of the paediatric oncologist Professor Richard Cohn. 'I would freak out in the weeks leading up. But nearly every time, Dr Cohn would shake his head in amazement and admire how well she was travelling. This made me feel really proud. So much so that sometimes I hoped I could run into a young doctor who had seemingly written her off from the outset just so I could smile and say, "Fuck you. Take a look at her now!"'

Aaron was regularly infuriated by the grim outlook they had once been given for Ainsley, back in the earliest days of her illness, by a doctor whose name he doesn't really remember. He still feels the frustration now. But it's no longer anger. It's pride, dressed up as indignation, from a heart swollen with joy.

Anger – pure anger – is reserved. A time and reason enough for rage was to come, when the anguish of caring for a daughter with cancer was replaced by the torture of an unimaginable tragedy. Because Ainsley de Jong could dance.

She could dance. She could sing. She could draw people in. And she did so for almost eight years, until 17 October 2014. On an otherwise ordinary Friday afternoon, Ainsley died – suddenly, inexplicably – in a packed, near-silent hospital emergency ward in front of her family … after an incident in the school playground.

'I didn't want her to die in hospital. She hated hospital,' Amanda says.

There, extended family were gathered near her bed in silence, while nurses and doctors worked on Ainsley. Watching. Waiting. Hoping. Praying. All sweating on a miracle that wouldn't come.

Eventually, Amanda realised that after seven years, ten months and one week of giving life everything, Ainsley had given her all. She'd given her last.

And so, a mother stepped forward and uttered what no parent should ever have to: 'I said to Dr Pretty, "She's gone through enough. That's it." He motioned to everyone. They stopped. And it felt like the whole hospital shut down. It went dead quiet.'

A world closed.

~

In her short life, Ainsley had spent an enormous amount of time in hospitals, fighting for her life – for the right to live, laugh and be loved. She had defied death when the odds were stacked against her. And now, death had come for her in a manner so unexpected, so unfathomable, it was shattering.

'She went through so much, it felt so unfair for her to be taken this way in the end,' Aaron says.

The anguish of Ainsley's parents runs far deeper than it should, saddled as it is with the burden of forever wondering, how does this happen?

How does a little girl go to school and not come home? Hit her head in a playground, go to hospital in an ambulance, and breathe her last not long after the bell has sounded at schools everywhere, sending other children home to their families?

And barely a sound is raised.

'The lack of change in the matters that resulted in her death, the lack of clarity and fairness in the courts, and the lack of real-life practicality and understanding in the systems that are meant to be fair and just make me feel like nobody cared,' Aaron says. 'But for me, this isn't about the school, the courts or the system. This is about my girl. This is about ensuring people know exactly what happened. It's about giving value to her life and it's about reaching out to the people that can make a difference … for her sake.'

This is Ainsley's story.

Autopsy Report (extract)

Dr Allan David CALA, 8 December 2014

Name: ***Ainsley Margaret DE JONG***
Post mortem no: ***141299***
Age: ***7 years (d.o.b. 07.12.06)***
Time & date of autopsy: 9am on 21st October 2014

AUTOPSY FINDINGS

EXTERNAL EXAMINATION:

The body *was that of a well-nourished female that weighed 22 kilograms and measured 110cm length.*
The scalp hair *was brown and 20cm length.*
The face *was broadened as was the forehead.*
There was slight 'bossing' of the forehead.
The neck appeared normal.
The eyebrows and eyelids *were normal.*
The eyes, sclera and conjunctivae *were normal.*
The irides *were brown.*
The cornea *were translucent.*
The nose *was normal. The nostrils were clear.*
The ears *were normal in shape and size and the meati were normal.*
The lips, gums and frenulum *were normal.*
The teeth *were normally erupted for age, and were normal although two upper left incisor teeth were absent.*
The chest, abdomen and back *were normal.*
The genitalia *were those of a normal infant female.*
The upper and lower extremities *bilaterally were well developed and symmetrical.*
The digits *were normally developed and nails and creases were unremarkable.*
The skin *was normal with no evidence of jaundice, tumour or rash.*
There was normal skin turgor.

CHAPTER 2

Nobody knew what to say

AINSLEY WAS A sister before she was born, a twin in the womb with a little boy alongside. It was news that delighted her parents and, very quickly, their extended family early in 2006.

'I was rapt, over the moon,' Amanda says. 'I remember driving back from Albury when we found out, and ringing the family. We were only six weeks in but I remember ringing and they were like, "What?!" "Yeah, we're having twins!" I was saying.'

The de Jongs live in Wagga Wagga, in southern New South Wales. Situated halfway between Sydney and Melbourne, the city is 50 kilometres off the Hume Highway, at the eastern end of the Sturt Highway, which carries traffic to Adelaide. But, four years into Amanda and Aaron de Jong's marriage, the Olympic Highway from Wagga Wagga to Albury had become the road that mattered most to them.

Despite living in the biggest inland city in New South Wales, the de Jongs had to travel an hour and a half south to the city on the Victoria–New South Wales border for IVF treatment as they sought to start their family. They were up to their eighth round, some $80,000 later, by the time the exciting news arrived.

'I just took the IVF as, this is something we have to do,' Amanda says. 'But it was a long process, an expensive process. And it was draining, emotionally draining. It took a few cycles, and then when it did happen, it didn't work. And there were trips back and forth from Albury …'

Aaron freely concedes that his patience began to be tested. As the months and years rolled on, he came to question whether they'd ever get to a stage of life he might have taken for granted.

'Early on, when Amanda wasn't falling pregnant, I wasn't too bothered,' he says. 'Then when we started IVF, I started really thinking, "What if we don't have kids?" As it kept going, I was getting really frustrated and really angry. Some idiot would say, "My husband just looks at me and I get pregnant" and I'd want to tell them where to go. The day I found out we were having twins was easily the best day of my life.'

Now, 2006 seems so long ago. Yet Aaron and Amanda's memory of their excitement at what it meant to be starting their own family is almost as fresh and thrilling as it was at the time. But the 17 years since *is* a long time. A lifetime. For the de Jongs, it is in fact two lifetimes, and then some. And none of it has been easy.

Amanda's pregnancy with twins was, for the most part, close to normal. However, around seven months into the pregnancy, their doctor noticed one of the twins was slightly smaller than the other. The couple was sent to Canberra for scans. Naturally, it was a big concern. But their fears were allayed when they were given the all-clear and reassured there was nothing to worry about.

'A month later, a few weeks before Amanda was due to give birth, we went for a scheduled scan and were hit with the news that there was only one heartbeat in the uterus,' Aaron says. It was beyond heartbreaking. It was incomprehensible.

'I obviously hadn't been pregnant before so I didn't know movement, I didn't know what to expect,' Amanda says. 'When we'd got to Canberra they basically said, "There's nothing wrong here. One's smaller but they're still thriving, everything's fine." Within weeks, he was gone.' She and her husband would have to farewell an infant as soon as they welcomed him into the world.

'I'll never forget the look on Amanda's face,' Aaron says. 'The heartbreak and disbelief. Tears ran down our faces and we were silent for what seemed like a very long time.'

Tears, it turned out, were to be a regular companion on their journey as parents. But in that moment, perhaps they understood, too, the true meaning of the opposite of sadness: the value they would place in fun, in laughter, in the joy and pride they would experience as parents.

~

The following weeks were confusing and sometimes unsettling as the couple tried to come to grips with the brutal reality of what lay in store.

'There was the excitement for the birth of our first child, yet a sense of devastation and grief about the death of our other child,' Aaron says.

On 7 December 2006, Amanda gave birth to their twins via caesarean and the midwives delivered Ainsley first.

'When Archie came out he looked good: pink … and healthy. Unlike Ains, who was covered in vernix and slightly blue,' Aaron remembers. 'His head was a bit squashed, and the doctor found a twist in his umbilical cord about 50 millimetres from his belly and assumed that's why he died. We didn't have an autopsy but with the benefit of hindsight, I wish we had.'

Aaron felt helpless. Frozen. Flat. Confused. It was almost impossible to take in. While Amanda was stitched up, he sat with Ainsley. And little Archie was wheeled away.

~

Amanda was reeling in the wake of her surgery, overwhelmed with the emotion of being a new mother and, at the same time, in a state of shock at having had her little boy Archie delivered without breath. Thank heavens for nurses who can sense a moment and deliver small mercies with the quietest of touch.

'I remember them saying they'd bring Archie in and I said, "No, no." I just kind of pushed it out of my mind,' she says. 'I felt a bit weird about it. That's my big regret, I didn't take him into the room with me and Ainsley at first. But I'm grateful to the nurse because she wheeled him in next to me and walked out. That was beautiful. It was beautiful she did that. Then we picked him up, held him, and I had him for a couple of nights.'

Aaron, too, was overwhelmed with gratitude when his little boy was brought back to them in the plastic hospital bassinet. But the following days weren't easy.

'People came to visit and it was just a really sad, awkward time,' he says. 'Nobody knew what to say. Archie was in the corner of the room next to Amanda's bed and most people didn't even realise. Not knowing what to do in that situation was the worst feeling. He slept in bed with us for a couple of nights and, while the time together with him was nice, the night the funeral director came to get him was really tough.'

And so it was that the de Jongs, parents at last, were immediately planning a funeral. A connection through Aaron's time as a local footballer helped ease the way.

'We were very lucky the funeral director was a bloke I'd known for a while through footy. John Bance is his name. An absolute gentleman,' Aaron says. 'I will never forget the night he came and took Archie away. He brought in a material bassinet and I remember it felt so nice and warm. We had a double bed in the hospital and we just stayed there in silence and cried for hours.'

Some of that first week is a blur for Amanda. But to see their little boy head out of the hospital room – alone – on his own final journey was devastating.

'I do remember him being taken away. That was awful,' she says. 'It felt like he was taken away in a suitcase – it was a bassinet but it had a zip.'

Amanda and Ainsley were discharged from hospital on the morning of Archie's funeral.

Aaron and Amanda had carefully chosen a plot for Archie at the Wagga Wagga Lawn Cemetery, opting for one that would be big enough for themselves when their time came. To lie forever alongside their little boy.

'It probably sounds a bit weird but when it came down to it, that's what we wanted – a plot to fit Amanda and me as well so we could all be buried together,' Aaron says.

On that warm day in December, the new parents headed from the maternity ward to the cemetery where they would say a final goodbye to their little boy, holding down for a moment all the worry and excitement that comes with having a bundle of newborn joy. And that was the way it would be for some time to come.

The days are long and the years are short, it is said, for parents of young children. For Amanda, time took turns between standing still and flying by with the burial of one baby and the learning to be at home with another.

'To be honest, I don't think I properly grieved for Archie. I don't feel like I had the time,' Amanda says. 'Of course, I *thought* about Archie. I just don't think I grieved enough, or I didn't have the time to process it … it all happened very quickly.'

John Bance's son Scott helped with the service. Like his father, Scott had a manner and decency that helped the young parents through the day.

'It was only a small graveside service with close friends and family,' Aaron says. 'I remember at the end it was so quiet and awkward. Everyone just stood there. Amanda went up to every person there to hug them and I felt I had to go with her … it just felt weird and I couldn't wait to leave. I thought at the time, "This is so bad, surely it's as bad as things are going to get for us."'

~

In the years since, Aaron has often wondered about the little boy Archie might have grown up to be.

'I think about it a fair bit, especially at kids' sport when I see the other boys playing or when we'd go camping and see friends' kids all playing together,' he says wistfully. 'When Ainsley was alive, her birthday parties with all our family around would get me thinking about it a lot, too.'

On that summer's day in December 2006, when a new mum and dad, aunts and uncles, grandparents and just a few close friends gathered to say goodbye to Archie, not one of them could imagine that it would be Ainsley who'd join her twin brother in a family plot picked for her parents.

CHAPTER 3

Priceless!

AINSLEY DE JONG WAS picking flowers at lunchtime on the day she died.

A few hours later, having been pushed over at school, fallen backwards and hit her head, Ainsley's 'life was pronounced extinct at 3.50pm', her autopsy would starkly report.

Life, according to the *Macquarie Concise Dictionary*, has many definitions. It isn't only 'the term of animate existence, of an individual', 'a period of existence from birth to death'. Life is also 'animation, liveliness … effervescence, or sparkle.' It's 'one who enlivens'. These were the definitions that Ainsley epitomised. The definitions of her.

Years have passed since Ainsley's death but the thought of her still brings an instant smile to the face of Carol Cattell. She was one of the nurses in the paediatric unit at

Wagga Wagga Base Hospital, where Ainsley was a regular attendee for chemotherapy and other treatment. Memories of the time spent with her little patient always bring on a range of feelings.

'When I think of Ainsley, I think of total joy, happiness, fun, yet sadness as well,' Carol says. 'My first thoughts are of happiness, remembering her dancing, particularly to "Gangnam Style". No one could dance to that song like her! It was *priceless*!!'

The hit song of 2012 by the recording artist Psy was a favourite of Ainsley's. More than a decade later, at the mere sound of a few bars, Carol finds herself happily bopping along. That was the impact of the little brown-eyed girl with the brown-bobbed hair and fringe, and a personality all her own.

Over the years, Carol became so close to Ainsley and the de Jongs that she delivered the eulogy at Ainsley's funeral in 2014. Looking back, what stands out most in her memories of treating Ainsley – aside from the laughs and the warmth she brought forth – is the little girl's connection to those closest to her.

'I always smile when she is mentioned,' Carol says, 'as do all the other nursing staff. She brought me such joy. Seeing Ainsley was the highlight of my week, yet I know it wasn't hers. I loved watching her dance, especially on her way to the treatment room. She was happy when she danced. I loved her telling me about the little figurines that she found in the playroom. I loved how her "Dolly" was so special to her and I would laugh with her as she sometimes threw Dolly across the room.'

Ainsley's little black doll was, quite simply and very quickly, the equivalent of another daughter in the de Jong household. A constant companion and calming influence, Dolly was a warrior by Ainsley's side as she marched onward into the battles that life served up.

'She thought she was the Queen, sitting up in bed when she was an in-patient for a few days,' Carol says. 'She had everyone wrapped around her little finger. I remember a brave little girl who was always polite and was most comfortable and secure when her family was by her side. Ainsley was happy when she was with her family. She trusted them all and often co-operated [during her treatment] with their support. I think she was brave and got through it all with her family's love.

'She understood the treatment routine and, honestly, I feel she responded to that, giving her the knowledge of what was happening with every visit. I hope I was able to give her that security so that she trusted me at least, just a little.

'I think of her every time I hear the two songs on the radio that were played at her funeral ['Gangnam Style' and '#thatPower' by will.i.am]. They make me sad. They remind me of such a sad day.'

Autopsy Report (extract)

Dr Allan David CALA, 8 December 2014

Name: ***Ainsley Margaret DE JONG***

Post mortem no: ***141299***

Age: ***7 years (d.o.b. 07.12.06)***

Time & date of autopsy: ***9am on 21st October 2014***

CIRCUMSTANCES OF DEATH

The information provided at the time of autopsy was taken from the police form P79a.

This 7 year old girl had been diagnosed with a pilocytic astrocytoma (a malignant brain tumour especially affecting children) at age 4 months. The tumour was known to have been based around the pituitary fossa at the base of the brain and was known to have spread throughout the nervous system with spinal metastases present.

She had undergone surgery followed by chemotherapy and radiation therapy at Sydney Children's Hospital, Randwick, and was under the care of an oncologist in Sydney. She last underwent chemotherapy treatment two weeks prior to her death. She had severe visual impairment and moderate intellectual disability.

At the time of her death, she was attending Willans Hill School in Wagga Wagga. This is [a] school which caters for children with intellectual and other disabilities. She had been residing with her parents and siblings in the family home at Wagga ...

CHAPTER 4

Sunlit sadness

YELLOW WAS AINSLEY'S favourite colour. The colour of sunshine and daffodils, a full moon and evening stars, funny cars and happy bikes and fields of canola flowering in spring. But the sun was out of sight – and so was joy – when the wind whipped up a horrible day in the spring of 2014 as hundreds gathered in shock to farewell Ainsley at a suburban Wagga Wagga church.

Funerals are rituals that help us cope with the upheaval of death, a scaffold that helps us through the earliest days of loss when it can feel like structure is required, not just to hold us together but – seemingly, surely – to stop the world from collapsing in on itself.

The saddest of days soured further by the minute as a gale blew outside and the weather threatened to do anything as a storm loomed. Then the clouds above the church parted just a little and sunshine suddenly and briefly illuminated the service. The narrow shaft of light speared into this room of mourning and scattered its glow in a widening cylindric path towards the floor, lighting up the particles and imperfections in the air. And every speck of dust lit up like all the sunsets and sunrises in a seven-year-old's life. Yellow light set the scene but the dust and matter created the beauty, forcing the light to show itself, to be seen.

The setting for Ainsley's funeral service was a church on the grounds of a Catholic primary school in Wagga, almost precisely halfway between the suburb in the city's north-west where her mother grew up and the south-eastern outskirts where her father was raised.

At seven, Amanda Kelly had been an old-fashioned little 'tomboy' in a household where her mum, Margaret, made sure they knew the value of family and of always supporting each other. Amanda was sporty and spent her spare time riding her bike and playing with Matchbox cars, before growing into a keen young basketballer who would also play football with her five brothers and sisters.

Aaron de Jong was a self-described 'little fat kid' madly riding motorbikes with his older brother and developing a passion for soccer. From the example set by his parents, he learned the importance of hard work and developing the drive to do your best.

Now Amanda and Aaron were parents and in the most unnatural and unfair position parents can be: burying a child.

It was a pre-pandemic world. The concept of 'pre-existing conditions' and associated questions about the value of a life would be publicly explored and widely debated at the start of the next decade, with the eruption of COVID-19 around the globe. As the coronavirus spread through unvaccinated and unprepared populations in 2020, it was almost common to hear it had claimed a life 'but the victim had underlying health conditions'. It begged the question: can a pre-existing condition be allowed to cheapen the value of a human life?

For the de Jongs, that most intimate of questions would rear its head over and over again in the wake of Ainsley's passing. After the sudden loss of a daughter who had stared down death any number of times before, they kept hearing themselves saying, over and over by way of explanation: 'Yes, she had a tumour. But no, the cancer didn't take her. She was fighting that. She was doing well.'

~

Denial and anger are the first two steps of the so-called stages of grief, famously introduced by Dr Elisabeth Kübler-Ross in 1969. But the original work of Kübler-Ross wasn't about grieving for someone who is gone. Denial, anger, bargaining, depression and acceptance were stages she identified for people who were themselves dying, and in the process of facing up to their own mortality. The stages offer some framework for the emotions a grieving person might face. But it's better understood now that grief is not a linear process. There are no five gates you pass through as you ski down the mountain of grief towards a finishing line marked 'return to normal'. Or 'closure'.

Dr Pauline Boss, a world-renowned therapist and pioneer in studying ambiguous loss, says it's simply not feasible to think that 'if you start with stage one and you move on through stage five, you're done … you're no longer grieving'.

'We now know that this is not true,' Boss says, 'and that human beings live with grief and, in fact, are able to live with grief. They don't have to get over it.'

In a world and culture focused on finding solutions to problems, it can be hard to accept the unacceptable. Simply working out how you'll go on is the real question. Critical to that, according to Boss, is the search for meaning in a loss. When death is inexplicable, finding meaning is that much more difficult. Boss says it's important to recognise there is a difference between clinical depression and the sadness of the grieving.

The cure for sadness, she says, is human connection.

Yellow

I rode a yellow bike today
Wheeled to yellow moon.
I yearned to taste a yellow sun
To eat with yellowed spoon.
I watched a cow chew yellow hay
And swept with yellow broom.
I lived in fear of yellow mood
Departing all too soon.
I felt a stream of yellow light
Like bright wool on a loom
Eyes closed I wondered at the sight
That yellow could entomb.
I shuddered as a yellow night
Shone on shadow's womb
Wondered if a force of might
Could shatter yellow's bloom.

Peter Doherty, 2023 – for Ainsley

CHAPTER 5

Days, not hours

'GRIEF,' IT'S BEEN said, 'doesn't care what kind of scene it enters. It just enters.'

Tragedy is the master of its own course; it marches to the beat of its own drum. What has already happened has happened, what's to come will come, and fate doesn't take fairness into account, nor consider what might be enough for a heart to bear.

In late 2006, with their treasured infant Ainsley, Amanda and Aaron de Jong hoped to find comfort in settling in at home as a family. The new parents planned to work through their pain of losing Archie while celebrating the new chapter of life they'd been sweating on for years.

'I couldn't believe how you can just love something so much in an instant, without knowing or spending time with them,' Aaron says. 'She was so precious, and she was all ours.'

At home, things were fine to begin with. However, Ainsley wasn't growing particularly quickly, sparking a little concern as she hadn't put on a lot of weight in her first weeks. She was sleeping a lot, too. Perhaps too much, Amanda would occasionally think. But none of this was any more a worry for the de Jongs than for anyone else at home with a baby for the first time.

After a couple of months though, Ainsley started vomiting heavily, sometimes projectile vomiting. Hopes of a happy start to their family life were to be shattered, again.

'It was unpredictable and a couple of times she screamed like she had been bitten by something or stabbed with a pin,' Aaron says. 'We weren't terribly worried but as first-timers with no idea what we were doing, we decided to book her in to see a doctor. We were instructed to change the formula, among other things … same stuff they tell everyone.'

A couple of weeks passed and little had changed. Aaron and Amanda were referred to a paediatrician. That's when they met Dr Joseph Moloney, a remarkable man who, upon his retirement some five years later, would be honoured with a mayoral reception in Wagga Wagga for his services to the city as a paediatrician for some 30 years. The de Jongs came to know him well. More to the point, he got to know Ainsley well, in his own inimitable style.

'When Ainsley was sick [later], we'd go and see him. We'd be the only ones in the waiting room and he'd come crawling out on his hands and knees,' Aaron recalls with a smile. 'She might be over playing with the toys and things and he'd just lie on his back in the middle of the waiting room, and start whistling and look over to see what she was doing. He was an odd rooster!'

In their experience, Moloney was all for the child, searching for a connection. With parents, he was a straight shooter, and Aaron and Amanda appreciated that. But late on that Thursday afternoon before Easter in 2007, with a trip to the New South Wales South Coast planned with Aaron's family, the couple didn't know who it was they were seeing, let alone that it would spark an immediate medical emergency, and a years-long association.

'The appointment was at 5 pm and we were keen to get going,' Aaron says. 'This was also the case for the office lady, who was also heading away for the weekend, so I paid the bill before we went in. As soon as we walked into the consultation room, Dr Moloney looked at Ains in an unusual manner.'

Next, the light in his ophthalmoscope wasn't working. The doctor looked a little edgy to the de Jongs. He abruptly departed the building for a nearby service station, returning with batteries. Aaron clearly remembers what happened next.

'He looked in her eyes and then commented, "Not to panic too much." He said, "We've got days not hours." He turned to his phone, picked it up and called the

CareFlight helicopter. Simple as that,' Aaron says. 'Not for the first time that afternoon, we were left questioning what was happening. The doctor then explained her symptoms: "Big head, vomiting and sunsetting eyes." All of these were being caused by pressure in her head.'

Amanda remembers hearing 'sunsetting eyes' and wondering exactly what that meant. At the mention of the large head, she tried to lighten the mood.

'I made a joke out of it. I said, "Well, look at Aaron's!"'

Moloney wasn't laughing.

'He went, "Oh! No, no." He was dead serious,' Amanda recalls. 'He was worried. He said, "There's pressure and we need to scan." He said, "Straight over to the hospital," and he was on the phone to Sydney before we left the room.'

Aaron remembers Moloney having a purpose about him that day, a seriousness that sent a scare through a young father. Within minutes, they were at Wagga Wagga Base Hospital, where Amanda and Ainsley waited for the CareFlight helicopter.

Aaron rushed home, packed a bag – including any Easter eggs they had – and, with his parents, Arthur and Lynne, and sister, Emma, set off on the 450-kilometre drive to Sydney. They arrived at the hospital in Sydney around 4 o'clock in the morning, almost exactly the same time as his wife and child on the chopper.

'There wasn't much talking in the car,' Aaron says.

It was a drive of anxiety and urgency as they powered

through into the early hours of the morning. Some of the little things have stayed with Aaron.

'Dad and I kept looking up at the sky to see if we could see the helicopter,' he remembers. 'We had an old-school sat nav and when we got to Sydney, my mum and sister put in the directions. It comes up with a button that asks if you want to avoid the tolls. They accidentally pressed yes so it took longer than it should have. It didn't matter, we still got there before Amanda and Ains. It's just something I remember. Arriving at the hospital, I still had in my head that it wasn't going to be that bad.'

Aaron remembers Ainsley being thrilled about her trip, eyes wide with glee as she babbled and chirped with excitement, as lively and loud as they'd ever seen her. He smiles now, at the memory of it.

'Ains was in the best mood after the helicopter ride. I remember her talking gibberish as she shared her story of flying. All this baby babble coming out, it was something she'd never done before.'

It helped him remain positive.

'Yeah,' Aaron assured himself. 'She may have something wrong but I'm sure they can fix it.'

~

Amanda, too, kept her composure. She held onto the thought that they were in good hands. That whatever it was, exactly, that ailed their daughter – a day shy of four months old – they were with the right people, and those people would find a solution.

'I felt like we just had to get to Sydney and find out what's going on,' Amanda says. She was pleased to be in the hands of NETS, the Newborn and paediatric Emergency Transport Service, a statewide emergency service for critically ill newborns, infants and children in New South Wales.

'Everyone was so lovely in NETS, they were amazing. They were talking me through it, and encouraging me to look out the window and take in the lovely scenery. I don't remember having a major panic until we were in Sydney and we finally got the diagnosis. I think that's when the seriousness of it all hit me.'

After scans, Ainsley's parents were informed she had hydrocephalus, a build-up of fluid on the brain that required a shunt to drain it.

'Hearing that was really upsetting,' Aaron says.

It was only the beginning. The little family from Wagga waited a couple of hours before a man in a suit arrived.

'I'm Ainsley's doctor,' he started.

The curtain was drawn and the doctor began by explaining the extreme size of the tumour in Ainsley's head. This was a shock to Amanda and Aaron.

'I was confused and was quick to question exactly what tumour he was referring to,' Aaron says.

The gentle Dr Kwok, in his suit and tie, and the nurse accompanying him immediately understood that they were talking to parents who hadn't been fully informed.

'They quickly realised we didn't know this and moved us to an office,' Aaron says.

Amanda says they were taken aback but still, her hope persisted. After all, they were in the medical system – a place where problems are solved – and surely now they'd be told how this issue was going to be fixed?

'They basically said you probably won't take her home. Or at least prepare …' She pauses. 'To not … take her home.' Amanda felt the anger building.

'I was like, "Are you fair dinkum? That's not going to happen!" The neurologist didn't seem positive at all. And then there were meetings to see what would happen.'

The tumour was the size of a golf ball – massive in a baby's brain. Ainsley's parents learned that was only half the problem.

'In your brain, you can have hard tumours that grow and when they grow everything around them just gets pushed out of the road and that's what causes all the trouble,' Aaron says. Those benign tumours are life-threatening, but they tend to grow slowly, and have defined boundaries. Ainsley's was not benign. It was malignant.

'Hers was a soft one so, as it grew, everything entangles in it. So you can't just go and cut it out. Because you'll cut out part of the brain,' is how Aaron remembers the explanation.

For the first time in his life – but certainly not the last – Aaron felt the ground shift under his feet and the world swirl around him.

'It felt like something you would see in a movie: everything started moving in slow motion,' he says. 'People's mouths around me were moving but I couldn't hear a thing and my vision developed a fog around it. The doctor and nurse went to get chairs for Amanda and myself. That was the first time I had ever had a feeling like that. The physical effects were scary. You think you've felt extreme emotions when good and bad things happen in your life but not like this.

'We were both in a bad way and the next thing I remember was being in a boardroom of doctors, nurses and social workers, discussing what they were going to do for Ainsley. It was surreal.'

Reflection from 'Omie' and 'Op'

Tears come to our eyes the moment we think of Ainsley, accompanied by the shock of remembering she is no longer here. It makes us cry, but then we smile.

Ainsley was very much her own person. She was wary of strangers and new people but she had an infectious laugh and she could keep it up forever. We just loved being with her.

Every Thursday she had a sleepover in our bed. She would slide out of the bottom of the bed and go to the playroom, and we would turn on the TV for her at all hours of the day and night. She loved watching Hi-5 *and dancing. She loved to hear Arthur make the sound of a duck.*

When we went shopping, we'd have to go to The Reject Shop every time, even if we didn't need anything.

The sad times were when she had to go to Sydney for chemo. But she didn't know that wasn't normal as she'd been doing it almost since she was born. We don't think she felt there was anything wrong with her. She never showed any distress about her sickness and treatment.

The saddest part of Ainsley's illness was watching Aaron, Amanda and the girls' heartache and us, as parents and grandparents, not being able to do anything to help make it better.

We think about Ainsley every day, and she's with us every day in all the photos around our house.

Rainbows remind us of her.

The colour yellow reminds us of her.

The song 'Gangnam Style'.

And Dolly – she was our fifth granddaughter.

Ainsley loved throwing little white rocks out of the gardens and then bringing them inside. We'd say, 'What does Op say?' And she would say, 'Don't throw rocks!'

She loved little toys rather than big ones, little soldiers and plastic animals. And saying 'farty bum' when someone did a fart.

We would take her to the coast with us and go on walks and she would only go one way. She didn't like to turn around and go back.

The sadness of her passing is no different today than it was the day she died. It has left us with a big hole in our hearts.

Lynne and Arthur de Jong, Ainsley's grandparents

CHAPTER 6

Whatever it takes

Five years into their marriage, Aaron and Amanda had been parents for only a few months and had already been through more challenges than many, including laying one child to rest. Now, here they were in Sydney, surrounded by specialists, wading through meetings about what might happen next to their little girl. Then came the waiting as Ainsley went into surgery for a delicate eight-hour operation. They were taken to a room and encouraged to try to get some sleep, reassured that if anything happened, they'd be contacted immediately.

'I sat at the door the entire time waiting for her to return,' Aaron says. 'My mind raced: "How had this happened?"'

Time became meaningless. Space – to move, to think, to breathe – was unsettling. The day seemed to take forever, and long, drawn-out meetings can be recalled word-for-word years later. Yet the hours also seemed to simply disappear.

'The day was so long but so fast,' Aaron says. 'I think we were still pretty naive or just uneducated in that short period of time as to how bad it was.'

The pair tried to remain positive, their inexperience seemingly offering a false reassurance that the worst of scenarios usually happen in other people's lives.

'I still thought they would cut it out and she would be okay. You think, "The real bad stuff won't happen to me."'

~

Ainsley did her bit to lift the spirits of her parents as soon as she woke from her marathon surgery, despite emerging from her anaesthetic with her head wrapped in bandages, an enormous scar and a startling bruise around her right eye.

'She woke up smiling,' Amanda says. 'It was awesome. She had a big black eye, but she was smiling. And oh, a beautiful, *little* round head.'

The black eye was the result of Ainsley's optic nerve being nicked during the procedure, which left her blind in her right eye. And the change to the shape of her head was immediately apparent.

'That was the first thing we noticed,' Aaron says. 'We felt a bit bad – we hadn't realised how swollen her head was. Now, she looked significantly different. It gave us a greater understanding of how much pressure there must have been in her head. But due to the nature and size of the tumour, doctors could only get ten per cent of it.'

~

Ainsley recovered in intensive care for a week, where the contrast between effort and environment struck Aaron over and over again.

'The nurses in ICU do an amazing job,' he says. But 'it can only be described as a shit place to be. A couple of times a day a nurse yells for someone to "get the trolley", meaning a baby or young kid was about to be resuscitated. Both Amanda and I would put our heads down every time. These events would conclude with either the sound of a big sigh or the crying of a parent.'

Ainsley's ICU stay was positive. Her recovery was good. The hard part came back on the children's ward. There, the excitement of seeing their daughter emerge from an epic operation to ease the pressure in her head was soon swallowed up by new, heart-wrenching discussions about what lay ahead.

'I think the next meeting was about do we treat her, or do we just let nature take its course,' Amanda remembers. 'Thank God we decided to treat her. I mean, we knew, we said straight up, "Of course we're going to try to treat her."'

Amanda and Aaron knew their daughter.

'When she had come out smiling, I was like, "You are kidding yourselves, you know? She will fight this",' Amanda says.

They met Ainsley's oncologist.

'Professor Richard Cohn, the best in his field and an absolute gentleman,' Aaron says.

Alongside his wife, Aaron was even more emphatic about their decision as parents.

'We spoke over a few days about a plan moving forward but also had to discuss the idea of not treating Ains and taking her home to die.

'*This was never going to happen*,' he declares. 'Because of the type of tumour and where it was located, radiation wasn't an option. The doctors settled on a chemo protocol.'

Thrust into the chaos of finding out what was wrong with Ainsley, and what was needed to give her the best chance of putting it right, Amanda and Aaron still found that Archie was never far from their minds.

'I would wonder if he had a brain tumour also,' Aaron says.

'Ains' tumour was five centimetres big when she was three months old. So, it had started growing when she was inside. I still can't believe it wasn't picked up in ultrasound while Amanda was pregnant. The doctor brought Archie over to us as soon as he was born and showed us a little sort of twist in the umbilical cord about five

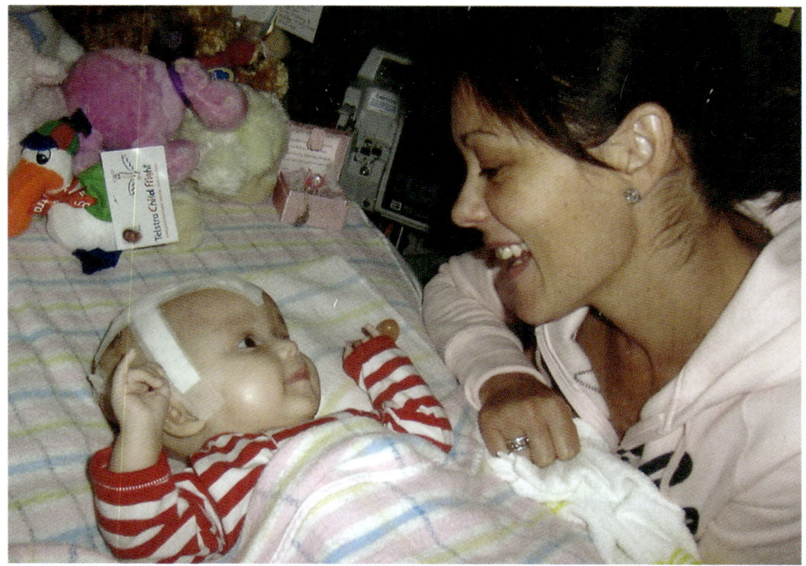

Ainsley and Amanda exchange looks of unadulterated joy a couple of days after her first major operation in 2007. Ainsley lifted the spirits of her parents when she woke up beaming following her surgery.

Aaron was rapt to have a new Geelong fan in the household and Ainsley was only too happy to be aboard the Cats bandwagon on AFL grand final day 2007. Geelong won the first of their three flags in five years.

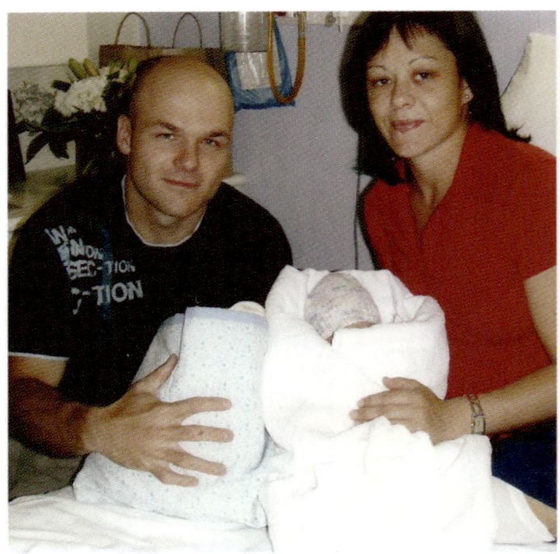

Aaron and Amanda with their twins Archie and Ainsley in December 2006.

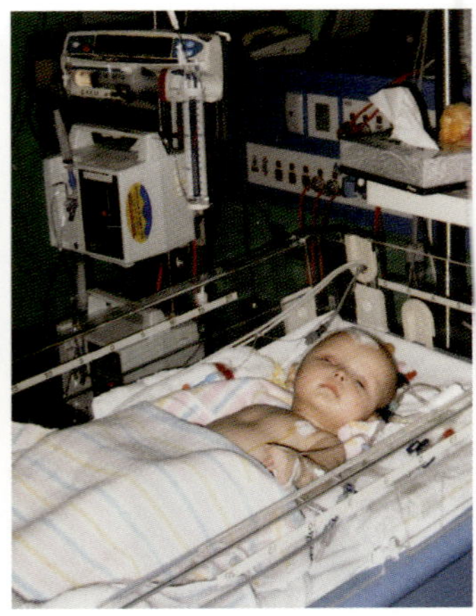

Ainsley the day after her operation in 2007.

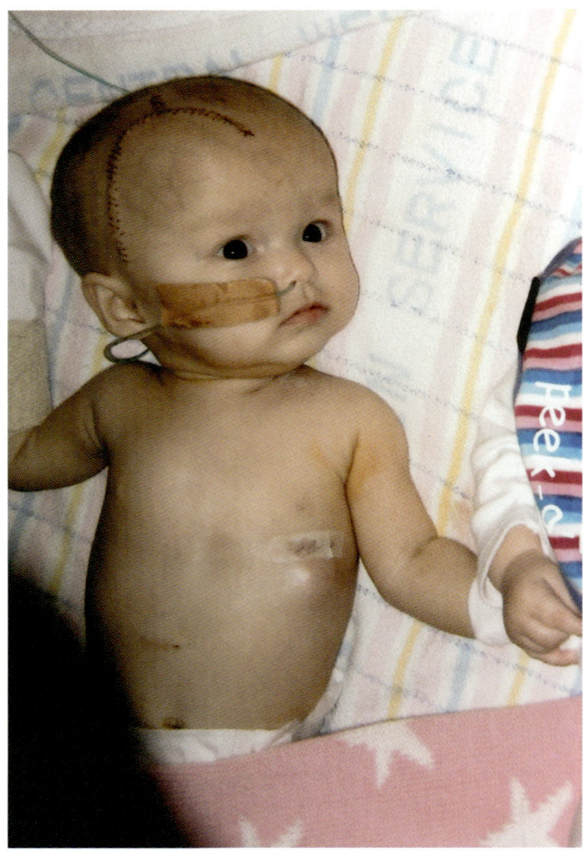

Ainsley at four months of age, bright-eyed and bearing the scars of battle, a week after her first operation.

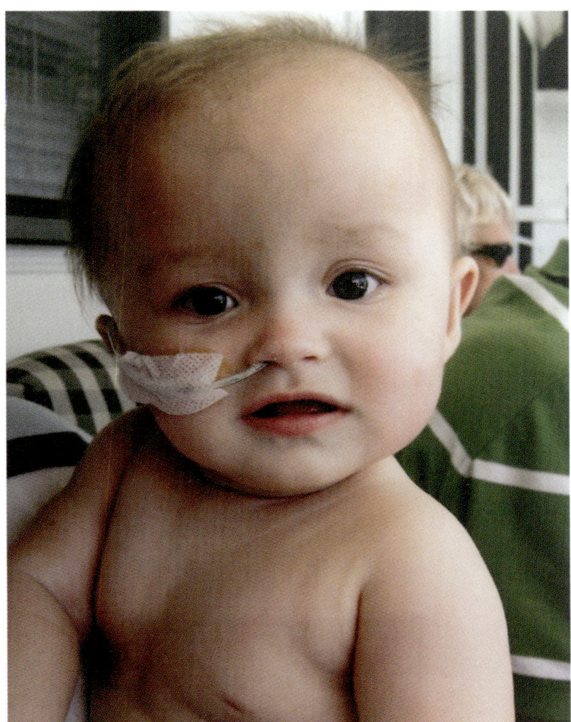

Ainsley feeling better during a break from her first round of chemotherapy treatment.

As a baby, Ainsley simply loved being in the water when she was well.

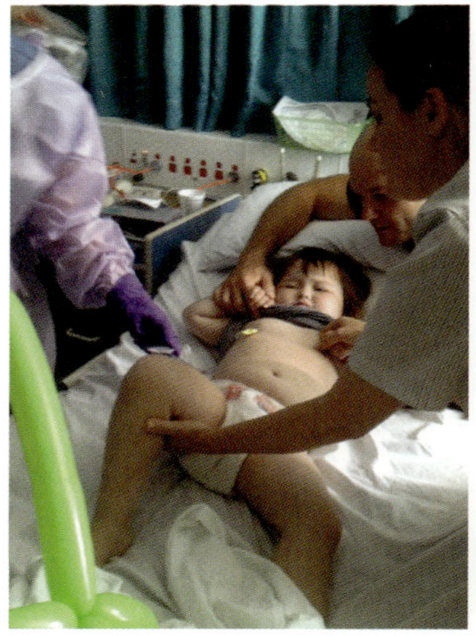

Chemotherapy treatments were almost a constant in Ainsley's life.

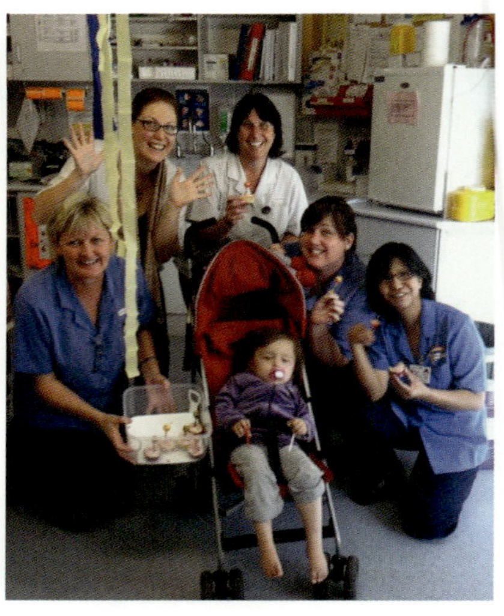

Celebrations after a final round of chemo for a while. Ainsley loved the support of her medical team, led by Carol Cattell (left).

Ainsley cute-as-a-button in a beanie, on one of the rare occasions she was willing to wear one.

Dressing up and showing off the look was never a problem for Ains though.

Ainsley and 'Omie' (her grandmother Lynne) getting ready to walk for charity together.

Aaron and Amanda with their three girls at Christmas in happier times.

A big moment: Ainsley struts in for her first day of school in 2012.

Addison and Ainsley.

Ainsley and 'Op' (her grandfather Arthur).

A look of joy receiving a mother's love.

The sisterhood: Ainsley with her little sisters Addison (left) and Audrey.

Aaron and Ains in a hospital waiting lounge.

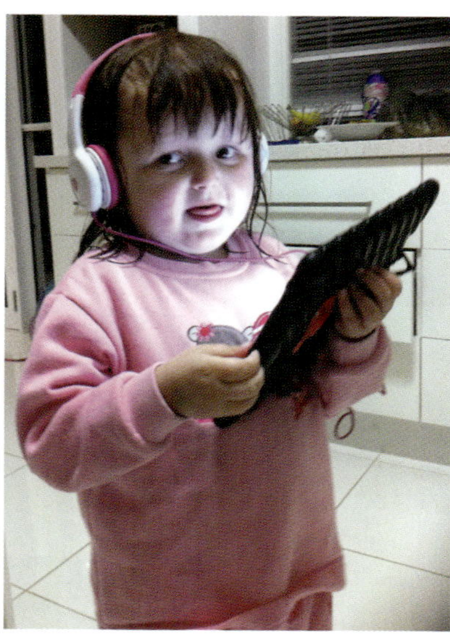

Ainsley simply loved listening to music.

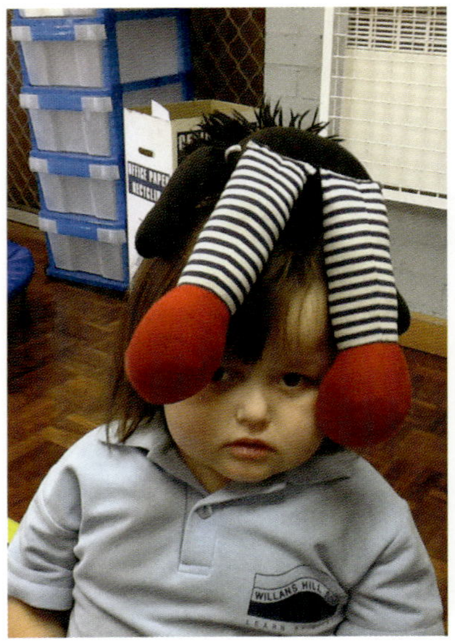

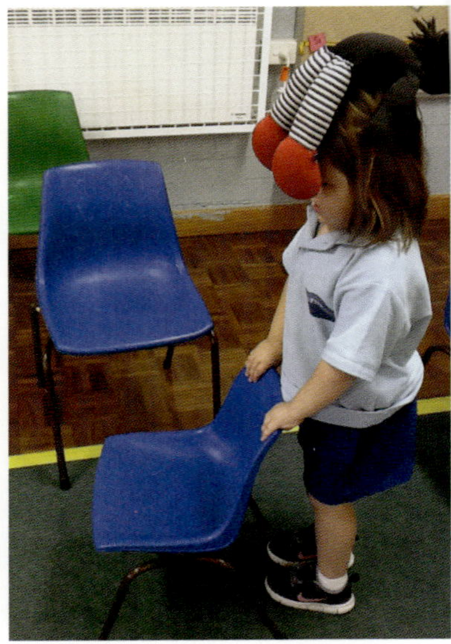

Ains and her beloved 'Dolly' were inseparable ... and hilarious!

Good times with Dolly helped Ains through happy school days (above) and testing times of treatment for her tumour (below).

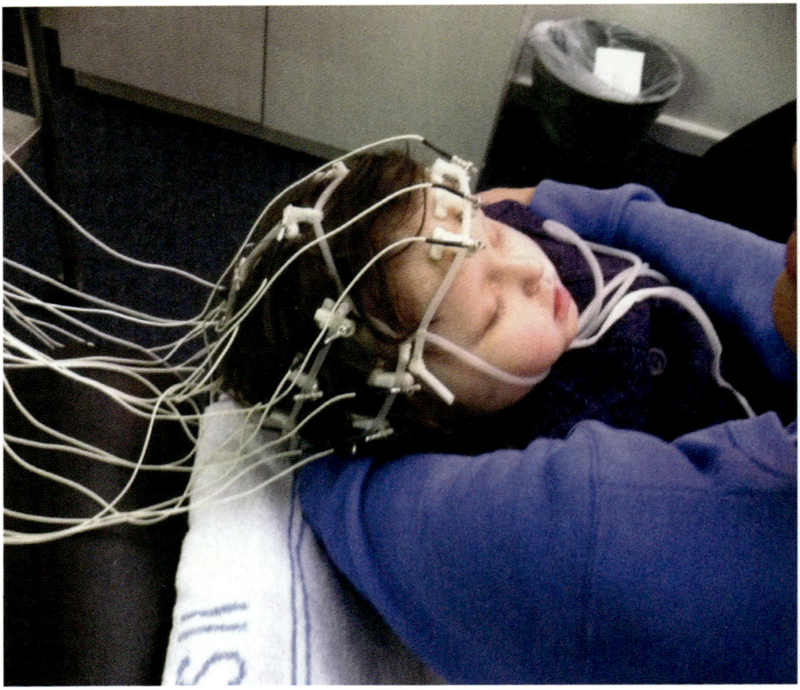

centimetres from his stomach and said that was probably the cause. It was so upsetting at the time, we didn't even think about an autopsy. Then when Ains got diagnosed the first thing they asked us was did we have an autopsy [for Archie]. They thought it would have been useful.'

~

The meetings were hard, the days were tough, and sleep was almost non-existent. When Aaron looks back, he can't quite comprehend how they even functioned that week, recalling how difficult it was simply to get his brain to think.

'People would always say, "I don't know how you did it", and I look back now and I don't know how we did it,' he says. 'You just had to. You had no time to deal with it. You're living your life one hour at a time, not thinking past that at any point.'

It might have felt as though their brains weren't functioning, but their hearts were running at full capacity. Almost unconsciously, love, instinct and passion drove them on, keeping the pair focused around the clock. Still, they never knew when the next shock was coming and certainly couldn't prepare for what form it might take.

'I remember being asleep on a chair early one morning and the surgeon's intern came in and woke me up,' Aaron says. He spoke about the surgery and commented that "their job had finished and it was now up to the forthcoming chemo treatment". He spoke about the "very hard road ahead for us and to prepare for bad things" that were going to happen. I didn't say a thing.'

This was the man whose comments would spring to mind for Aaron in the years to come, and forever serve as a lightning rod for a rush of anger and indignation.

The brief, one-way discussion was one of thousands that both men would be part of throughout their lives, but one of them will never forget it. To this day, Aaron doesn't know whether the intern was attempting to help, warning them to prepare for the worst, or simply chose his words poorly for the discussion at the time:

'I'm not sure if it was just the timing, and I was tired and cranky,' he says. 'Either way, I didn't care. My first thought as he walked out of the room was, "Fuck you, mate. We are going to do this. I'll back us in at one per cent and you can just fuck right off."

'No matter what the cost, we were going to do whatever it takes. I was thinking, "I can sleep on a chair for the rest of my life. I'd sell my house in an instant." Amanda and I are very competitive people and I think he doubted our resilience. I also had in my head that Ains was half me and half Amanda, so she was going to have a red-hot crack.'

Not surprisingly, Professor Cohn was soon aware that doing nothing wasn't an option for the de Jongs.

PART 2

The Music in Her

Ainsley de Jong, born with a song
Nestled deep in her heart
Ainsley de Jong, laughed loud and long
And everyone else would start

An ear for the beat, the dance in her feet
The music couldn't be wrong
Delight, unbridled, and love sidled
Right up to 'Ainsley the strong'

With a name meaning 'meadow'
Or 'a field of one's own'
Maybe Ains and her shadow,
Little Dolly, alone:

Dancing, singing, laughing and more,
Mischief meets mischief; laugh becomes roar
A place where spirits are inspired to soar
In this field of fun – good vibes galore.

Peter Doherty, 2023 – for Ainsley

CHAPTER 7

Bigger things to worry about

AMANDA KELLY AND Aaron de Jong were married in 2002. Aaron was a highly regarded jeweller and widely respected premiership-winning player with The Rock–Yerong Creek Football and Netball Club, where Amanda was a competitive and talented netballer.

Aaron's father, Arthur, had come to Australia as a child after the family fled the Netherlands with next to nothing during World War II. His mother, Lynne, also had a tough upbringing. She was raised by her wheelchair-bound mother, a polio sufferer who brought up her daughter alone after Lynne's father disappeared when she was a young girl, never to be seen by them again.

Arthur and Lynne met, married and created a happy and stable family of their own. Aaron arrived in between his older brother, Nathan, and younger sister, Emma.

As well as raising their kids, Lynne worked in numerous jobs, including a long stint as a nurse at an aged care home. And Arthur set a standard for hard work as he established a successful building business in Wagga Wagga.

'You'd always see Dad going to work at six in the morning. He always worked really hard. In school holidays, my brother and I would be on the job sites. Dad would be getting us doing something,' Aaron says.

Amanda's family life hadn't been easy. Her mother died of breast cancer soon after Aaron and Amanda were engaged, and Amanda did her best to support her siblings, Tanya, Jason, Nicole and twins Tamara and Nathan. The third of the six kids to parents Marcus and Margaret, Amanda was smack bang in the middle of her family. She grew up surrounded by cousins and extended family on her mother's side, in an environment where two important points were clear: 'Mum was one for family – you would always be there for family, be there for each other, without being in each other's pockets,' she says. 'And always do what you know is right. Don't look to please others.'

After school, Amanda worked in administration and accounts at Kendall Airlines, which became Rex Airlines, and later at Charles Sturt University.

Popular, personable and social, with a strong friendship group and part of a tight-knit football and netball community, the couple looked forward to creating a happy and harmonious family life of their own.

'I didn't really think much about having kids until my brother started his family,' Aaron says. 'I was too busy working. But it was all Amanda thought about once we got married.'

Aaron had enjoyed school but left in Year 10 to take up an apprenticeship as a jeweller. When his apprenticeship ended, he was offered the chance to become a partner. The once-relaxed teenager found he had real drive, and wanted to work as hard as he could to build the business and do well in his chosen profession. It was an approach he also developed towards sport, applying himself to his Aussie Rules – which had overtaken soccer as his favoured sport – enjoying team success and making representative teams.

Soon enough, the idea of starting a family with Amanda took hold.

'I knew the relationship I had with my parents was good and, I suppose if I did think about it, I thought it would be cool to have my own little human,' Aaron says. 'Sometimes I would think, I hope my grandkids tell people about me when they get older, even if it's just me doing something dumb or something they can laugh at. Maybe I was worried that I might be forgotten pretty quickly if I didn't have my own family.'

Parenthood is life-changing at the best of times. When Ainsley was diagnosed with a brain tumour, the once outgoing pair virtually gave up any idea of a social life to focus on their daughter. It wasn't that they didn't want to do much. They simply couldn't.

'Amanda and I still got invited to things for a while but after a few years people got sick of us saying we couldn't go and stopped asking, which was understandable,' Aaron says. 'To be perfectly honest, it didn't really bother me as we had bigger things to worry about. I had a few mates that didn't stop asking and still always ask now, which I really appreciate.

'Often I've found the people you didn't think would provide support sometimes become the ones who support you the most … some of them don't even know they are helping.'

That help from family and close friends was invaluable, because life for the de Jongs had changed. They now inhabited a different world. This was a universe populated by doctors and specialists; a place of meetings and medical terminology, prognoses and predictions; discussions about quality of life, and prospects. There were so many doctors. And so many types of specialists. That was something to be grateful for. But it's a place unfamiliar to the ordinary person and it was overwhelming to find themselves suddenly thrust into the centre of it.

'There are whole teams, but they're so specialised,' Aaron says, casting his mind back to Ainsley's treatment. 'There's the oncologist for cancer … the surgeon for the tumour … the neurologist for where to cut it and why to cut. You feel a bit like saying, "Mate, surely you know a bit more about what's going on than just your one area?",' he says with a smile. 'But he only tells you about his bit. And you've got all these experts in a room … you know … they all just do their one little thing. That's what surprised me. So every time you go back for a check-up, you've got to see six different doctors. They'll say, "Just come back tomorrow … we'll do that on that day, fit that in there …" They don't understand when you say you live in Wagga and it isn't that easy. There were always logistical nightmares with those things.'

Wagga Wagga is no tiny country town. It's the largest city away from the coast in New South Wales, with a population of more than 60,000. And, as a regional capital, it has services to cater for probably twice as many, taking into account the populations of surrounding towns. But being a five-hour drive from the state's capital city was an added burden, one that would seemingly haunt Aaron and Amanda years later when Ainsley was no longer with them.

For now, though, their focus was simply on what they had to face next. And – to be clear – they couldn't be more thankful for the medical help and support they received.

'We are so grateful,' Amanda says.

'In Sydney and Wagga, everyone was amazing. Most of the medical staff even came to Ainsley's funeral. They made a massive effort to come. I think Ainsley's treatment was spot on. I don't think anyone didn't do enough, or didn't care enough. And we were lucky with Wagga too, with Paediatric Outreach [a service of specially trained nurses to help treat seriously ill children in the region]. They did a lot here.'

~

Once Aaron and Amanda had set the record straight about their intentions and placed full trust in their little girl's opportunity to live her own life to the full, Ainsley began chemotherapy. It was just two weeks after the initial operation to reduce her tumour.

'She was good. She didn't react too badly, she wasn't too sick. She coped well,' Amanda says.

They explored all options, including meeting with the high-profile brain surgeon Charlie Teo.

'People said, "Go and see him, he's the best, he can do anything", blah, blah, blah, so we had to do it, obviously, to ask the question,' Aaron says.

The de Jongs already trusted the doctors they had, one of whom was in fact one of Teo's superiors. But no one discouraged them from looking at every other possibility, including Dr Teo.

'It was $500 cash to see him – for 15 minutes. The bloke in front of us at the rooms asked if they had EFTPOS. "No, there's an ATM out the front." That's what they told him, hahaha,' Aaron remembers.

Teo was straight with them about Ainsley's plight and the difficulties with her tumour. He had no miracle answers or offers. Aaron and Amanda appreciated his honesty. They knew Ainsley faced a difficult fight. They continued to back her, sticking to the agreed chemotherapy plan.

'We were shitting ourselves the first time,' Aaron says.

'The nurses entered in bright purple hazmat suits and Ains was asleep with a port already inserted in her body. It was cone-shaped and screwed to her ribs under her skin.

'This was so the chemo went in the right place each time she was treated. When the fluid went in, she squirmed and screwed up her face like she had a bad taste in her mouth.'

The de Jongs set up camp at Ronald McDonald House as Ainsley faced up to weekly treatment to begin with, later pushing out to fortnightly, with some scheduled breaks. And there were blood tests before every chemo protocol to determine if a little body could handle the next course. Aaron remembers too well the toll on their tiny daughter.

'The treatment smashed her white blood cell count and she was all over the shop,' he says. 'She'd be really sick and lethargic by the end of weekly chemo sessions, then be really good by the end of the breaks. Happy. At times, she was skinny, and then really fat.

'We were in Sydney for the first few months of her treatment and stayed at "Ronnie Macs", which is at the back of the hospital. This was really convenient but due to the nature of what they do, it can be an awful place to be.

Hanging around really sick kids can be tough. The kids usually have one parent being kind and trying to hold it together, while the other parent hates the world and wants to take it out on someone or something. I know which one I was!'

Six months into Ainsley's treatment, the family was able to go home and fly to Sydney regularly for treatment. It wasn't easy at home. Early on, it was downright scary, not to mention wearing on the young parents.

'We had to keep tube feeding Ains, every hour at one point,' Amanda says. 'I don't think we slept much. We were just making sure she ate. We had to hold the tube up and feed her. But it was nice. It was really good to be home.'

Each trip to Sydney was an ordeal in itself – up early, on the 6 am flight out of Wagga, organising vehicles with baby seats, attending appointments all day and into the evening, and tearing back to the airport in time for the last flight home. It didn't always go smoothly.

'One day we were running really late and couldn't get a cab with a baby seat,' Aaron says.

'The dodgy cab driver said we'd be fine if Amanda held Ains in the backseat. As we were driving to the airport, the cabbie did a U-turn and we were T-boned. We were okay – we were able to hail down another cab and got to the airport with time to spare – but on reflection, it was stupid.'

~

As Ainsley drew close to her first birthday, the de Jongs were able to continue her chemotherapy in Wagga. Here, they were privileged to cross paths with someone whose care and expertise they'll never forget.

'Carol Cattell was our nurse and put simply, she is amazing! The nicest lady you'd ever meet,' Aaron says frankly. 'If Ains got crook or had to have a blood transfusion or chemo, Carol did it. There were certainly other nurses who supported our family during this time, but Carol was there to support us every time. We became good friends over the years.'

Carol wasn't the only healthcare worker taken in by Ainsley's lively personality and heart-warming presence.

'When we went into the Base Hospital in Wagga, it felt like Ains was a celebrity,' Aaron says. 'She had so many visits from all of the hospital staff, particularly the nurses who would regularly end up dancing to 'Gangnam Style' with her. She loved the attention! When we went to Sydney, she was a bit of a celebrity there, too, always willing to put on a show … I've got so many videos! Hospitals are usually sombre sorts of places, where people having minor things done can be moping around like it's the worst thing that can happen. Then Ains walks in, like a rockstar, and no whingeing!'

~

That was Ainsley: bright and bubbly and taking it all in her stride, making friends and winning new fans along the way, despite the toll the treatment took.

'She was mostly pretty happy,' Amanda says. 'Over time, we noticed, when she had breaks from chemo, that she would be a lot brighter. You'd sort of go, "Shit, she wasn't very well back then. Look at her now!" So she obviously wasn't feeling great during it. But she coped.'

From Ainsley's Eulogy

Amidst the last five years of treatment, Ainsley was lucky enough to have two beautiful sisters to share her life with.

Addison and Audrey, you have been beautiful and gentle sisters.

You have been a really big help to Ainsley and we know how much you adored her. Ainsley loved you both and she was very lucky to have you both in her life.

Carol Cattell, Paediatric Outreach Nurse, Wagga Wagga Base Hospital
Sacred Heart Church, October 2014

CHAPTER 8

A big sister

AINSLEY MARGARET DE JONG had arrived as a 2.51-kilogram bundle of joy at birth, or five-and-a-half pounds in the old money. She was 48 centimetres in length. They're dimensions that can't come close to explaining the life contained within.

Ainsley took her time learning to walk. She walked on her knees for months before getting to her feet at the age of three. Her development was delayed by her condition. However, Ainsley was strong. She was determined. And she was resourceful.

'I think being half blind made her that way,' Aaron says. 'She got around slowly, almost gingerly, always looking around taking everything in when she entered a new room. She would stop at shadows a lot, not knowing if they were steps.'

Ainsley lived up to every expectation her parents had that she could battle a tumour. She would fight her cancer. Hell, she'd even fight the people trying to help her if she had to.

'Trying to hold her down at times for treatment often took a few people and she would not give up,' Aaron says, with more than a hint of pride. 'But by the end she would say in a happy sweet voice, "Thank you", and just made everyone feel good.'

Ainsley was, unashamedly, herself. She hated getting her haircut (but would sit for her Aunty Michelle). She didn't like ponytails and preferred not to have any ribbons in her hair. She was all personality.

After every course of treatment in Sydney, on the drive home, Aaron and Amanda couldn't help but lock eyes and give each other a knowing look – a look of unbridled pride in their spirited daughter and her combination of fight and fun as Ainsley kept on surpassing expectations, all the while lighting up the lives of those around her.

'Ains was autistic, and she had a lot of innocence and friendliness about her, which drew people in. Once she got your attention, she was very cheeky – innocently cheeky,' Aaron says.

Once she was up and going, Ainsley was rarely sighted without her iPad and, armed with Dolly by her side, this little girl, whose life had been on the brink as an infant, got busy winning people over.

'She made everyone smile and feel good. I think it was a combination of her upbeat personality and people knowing what she was going through,' Aaron says. She would often be having chemo and dancing and singing to *Hi-5* with nurses while eating Tiny Teddies. She would just make you laugh, shake your head and wonder: "How?"'

For all they'd already been through, and amid the chaos and intensity of the treatment, Aaron and Amanda simply loved having Ainsley at home. This little girl, who loved presents more than parties – 'It didn't matter what they were, she just wanted to unwrap them,' Aaron says – was creating the family life her parents had long hoped for.

'There are just a lot of enjoyable memories,' Aaron says. 'For a while, when she was little, before she could walk, every night she and I would lie on the floor together on this little pink couch she had and watch at least two episodes of *The Sopranos* together. Obviously she didn't understand it but it was nice just lying next to her. After a couple of weeks, she could hum the theme song.'

From her earliest days, it was always the tune, the beat, the dance, the song for Ainsley. She had the music in her. And mischief, too.

Amanda lets out a joyous laugh when she remembers what life was like at home with their daughter.

'She was hectic! Yep. She was hectic. When she didn't get things her way, she'd let you know.'

The home had stairs, which for some reason became Ainsley's preoccupation whenever the mood took hold. It wasn't in anger – just for fun – but Ainsley wanted to throw anything she could at that flight of stairs, from toys and cups to the kitchen cutlery and everything else she could lay her hands on. The knives and forks ended up being stored on a shelf around eye-height for adults, to be out of reach of clutching hands and an obsessive mind.

It was pure joy to have a taste of another life for a while: a couple at home with their child, learning the ropes of parenting for the first time.

'I think we got into a bit of a normal situation for a while. That's when I felt, whatever happens here, Ainsley needs a sibling. So, we went back down the IVF track,' Amanda says. 'While she was going well, I wanted to try for another one. I wanted her to have a sibling, whether it was for a long time or whatever.'

Addison arrived in December 2008 and then Audrey in August 2010.

To begin with, Ainsley wasn't sure about the arrival of Addison and the competition, with her personal space being occupied and her parents now shared. But they soon formed a tight partnership.

'She was horrible at first,' Amanda says, laughing again. 'Horrible! I think there was a bit of jealousy but once she worked out that she could get her sister to do stuff for her, then she and Addi formed this cute little bond. Addi was a slave, and Addi didn't complain! She did everything for her.'

Audrey's arrival upset Ainsley's world again, just as she'd started to work out a nice rhythm of service from her first little sister.

'When Audrey came along, Ains was terrible to her ... she just threw things at her. I couldn't leave Aud alone,' Amanda says. 'But what's lovely is we have a photo of Ainsley cuddling her and that's what Audrey remembers.'

Cuddles weren't really Ainsley's thing. She was a reluctant cuddler. It's what gives that photo with her sister so much meaning. Cheekiness was more Ainsley's go and she remained full of surprises.

Hearing tests were a regular part of her medical routine, to double check if the chemotherapy was having any adverse effect.

'It was always a nightmare, usually at the end of a few other appointments, and she would be over it before we got there,' Aaron says. 'But there was one time – and I have a video of it that I watch all the time – she walked in, said hi, kneeled up on the chair and put her headphones on. She wasn't told what to do. There was a jar of marbles in front of her and, when she heard a noise, she was meant to put a marble into a game. As soon as they started, she would mimic the noise and put the marble in and laugh. She smashed it. I cried all afternoon with pride. I still do when I watch it.'

~

Revisiting the past, there is such joy for Ainsley's family in remembering what she gave them. Aaron says, even in the tough times, life didn't feel difficult in the moment. It was simply life.

Now, looking back, he can be dragged into sadness, recalling when the frustration, the sheer complexity of all that they were facing, and the days without sleep – not even a wink – wore thin.

Still, they knew what it was for, and they learned the preciousness of time.

'I remember sitting in waiting rooms for four or five hours, and it was nothing,' he says. 'In my mind, I would think it doesn't matter where I am, at least it's time spent with her.'

Amanda, too, points out that perspective is everything.

'You hear people say they hate going to hospitals. I'd give anything to be back in hospital with Ainsley now. It's funny how life is. I would never have thought I'd miss it.'

Reflection from Aud

The first thing that comes to mind when I think of Ainsley is her having her strawberry milk Up&Gos. I would always finish it off for her. Also rainbows. When I look up in the sky and see a rainbow, I know that she is always with me.

I didn't really know Ains for long but I know she loved food and Dolly. She would not go anywhere without Dolly. She loved to dance. She loved The Wiggles. *And she gave everyone around her a really good vibe. She was always friendly.*

When I hear her name, it makes me smile because of all the memories I have of her and the positive vibes she would always bring to everyone. One of my favourite times with Ains was when we went to the footy and she was throwing green snakes around, all over the footy field.

Things that made me happy with her were dancing to The Wiggles *and* The Fairies. *Eating packets of snakes together. Just laughing and playing outside on the swings and in the cubby house with her.*

What made Ains happy was honey sandwiches, and Up&Gos. She loved her food. Toy Story *and* Dora the Explorer *were her favourite things to watch along with* The Wiggles *– they made her so happy. She loved the beach and throwing rocks on the road.*

One time, when we were about to go to bed, we were in Mum and Dad's room and she hugged me. Mum took a picture. I still miss her.

I think the way she handled everything was so brave and strong and she never gave up until she couldn't do it anymore. She would dance and sing even if she was in pain. I'm still so proud of the way she handled things and how everyone else did when she passed.

I think of Ains every day. She was so funny, and kind. When I lie in bed at night, I think of her and how brave she was.

I don't think her death changed me that much but it changed me growing up. Instead of being weak, I was strong and little things didn't matter to me as much because I know there are more important things.

I always knew there was something wrong with Ains. At the time I was too young to understand everything that was happening. Now that I'm older, I feel really bad about her past and I try to make Mum and Dad happy.

She was a really good sister. When someone talks about her past I can get really sad sometimes but I have learned that I can't change the past and that I can't change what happened but we can stop it from happening to someone else.

Audrey, Ainsley's youngest sister

CHAPTER 9

She will be safe here

TIME. ENERGY. HOURS. Days. Nights. Weeks. Months. Years.

Life rolled on in a hurry for the de Jongs, as it does for most young families. For a year or so from the middle of 2011, the sheer normality of it all was something to treasure. It is now, too. Not that it was entirely normal.

'We always knew the tumour wasn't going away,' Aaron says. 'We just embraced that break when things were good. But every three months we had to go to Sydney for that MRI of the whole body. And you're just sweating on it, you know?'

For six months on either side of Ainsley's fifth birthday in 2011, and again throughout 2013 and into 2014, medical emergencies gave way to birthdays, family events and the regular milestones of growing up for a family with three little girls at home. Amanda remembers clearly her eldest daughter's first day at school in 2012.

'It was a bit weird. She was tiny. I sat in the carpark and cried for a good couple of hours,' she says. 'I was worried. Just because she was so little. And that it wasn't a normal school. But her teachers were so lovely that they made you feel like, "This is okay." I knew that this was the next step to a normal kid's life. You've got to start school.'

Aaron and Amanda had flirted with the idea of a mainstream school for Ainsley. They visited a number of primary schools, checking out the facilities at each one, including their special needs hubs. During one visit, the couple was starting to seriously contemplate a regular primary school enrolment for their daughter … until the bell rang for recess.

'Kids came running from all directions,' Aaron says. 'Amanda and I looked at each other and quickly came to the realisation that Ains would get skittled within seconds. Choosing a school was a big decision for us. I had the attitude that if she hung out with kids who were more advanced, it might also drag her along more quickly. [Initially] Willans Hill School wasn't an option for me.'

Willans Hill School is a NSW Department of Education school classified as a School for Specific Purposes, specialising in supporting students with a variety of learning needs. Having recognised that mainstream education wasn't for Ainsley, Aaron and Amanda toured the school, just south of Wagga Wagga's business centre, across the road from the city's botanic gardens.

'We decided it would be best for Ains,' he now says. 'I remember telling the principal, Chris Lennon, the story about us visiting the public school and recognising it wasn't suitable after we witnessed the noise and chaos at recess. She told us not to worry. Her exact words were, "She will be safe here."'

Amanda draws in a wistful breath at that thought.

'In hindsight,' she wonders, 'I don't know. Somewhere else might have been better.'

But at the time, they *were* happy with their decision. They'd looked through the school grounds and its classes and certainly believed that Ainsley would be safe. It *seemed* as though it would suit. Not that Ainsley loved it from the start.

'Oh, I wouldn't say that,' Amanda chuckles. 'Some days you'd pick her up and she was happy. Other days, well … she may not have been well from her treatment, but she didn't want to be there.'

Her parents remember tantrums in the car on the way to school, when her clothes might come off and be flung around the car, or one of her sisters would be in the firing line.

'Just getting her there could be a pain,' Aaron says. 'She could be a nightmare. Amanda would pull up there and she'd be naked in the car, screaming and carrying on.'

One of the great sadnesses of a tragedy is the rear vision, continuing to look back, years on, and finding yourself questioning everything. What was possibly just part of the process for their autistic daughter growing accustomed to going to school can come back as haunting, potential signposts.

'I don't know if her actions were signs of things, like "Mum, this isn't …"' Amanda's words trail off. 'You know, she couldn't talk. I look back and think and wonder if they were signs. Was she saying, "Do not leave me here"?'

Despite the rigmarole of getting Ainsley to school, then out of the car and into class, her parents had every reason to be happy with the education their daughter was receiving.

'They took lots of school videos of her doing things and they would show us. She seemed happy doing them,' Aaron remembers. 'Once, we got to hide in the classroom, up the back. That was pretty cool, to see how she was at school.'

The parents stayed out of sight because if Ainsley saw them, she would want out. But without knowing they were there, Aaron and Amanda could see that she was happy and enjoying school.

'They were some really nice times, when we got to see her there. I worked in the canteen sometimes too, just to spy on her,' Amanda laughs.

But at the mere mention now of Willans Hill School, Amanda's heart skips a beat. Then she can feel it racing in her chest.

'It does. And then I quickly go back to being *very* grateful for what they taught her,' she says. 'I do feel that, even leading up to when she passed, she was just growing. She was able to communicate better with us, she was a little bit calmer. I thought she was going to be around forever. She was just doing so well, in everything.'

Aaron proudly remembers that it wasn't all that long before he was walking along the street and listening as his eldest daughter first pointed at and then read out loud the letters on shopfronts, and the numbers on car parks.

'It showed us she was getting smarter,' he says. 'She was doing things we thought she would never be able to do. They were great for her at the school.'

After Ainsley's death, the de Jongs heard talk of some playground incidents that they hadn't been aware of at the time, including suggestions that Ainsley might have been pushed over or shoved on a couple of occasions. But throughout her time at the school, they never had reason to worry.

There were days and weeks in 2014 when the de Jongs imagined, with real hope, that Ainsley's learning and progression might run for years to come. Still, her illness was always ready to issue a reminder. As it did on 30 July that year.

'On my birthday, I was sitting on the back deck with my family,' Aaron says. 'It had been a while since Ains had any sort of treatment and she was going strong. But on this day, I could see her walking down the hallway guiding herself along the wall with her hands. I got up and went to check on her and everything seemed all right, but Amanda and I quickly realised that she had lost her vision.'

They panicked, headed to hospital and were in Sydney by the next morning. Pressure had again built up in her head, so a tube was inserted to drain the fluid.

After the operation, Aaron, Amanda and Ainsley were in the room together. Outside, doctors gathered in discussion to review the procedure that had just been completed. That's when they saw their social worker, Catherine, arrive.

'Something that I've learned over time is that when the doctors are gathering to discuss something of this nature and your social worker turns up with them, it's a worry,' Aaron says. 'As Catherine made her way to the team of specialists, my heart sank. This time, however, it was just a simple coincidence. She was just walking past! We were quick to ask her never to turn up impromptu like that again when the specialists were meeting!'

Catherine is originally from Leeton, a town 125 kilometres north-west of Wagga Wagga. She had built up an excellent rapport with the de Jongs, who still laugh about the fact that, in the middle of a serious panic, they could share a joke about the circumstances.

As for the emergency, it turned out that the shunt between the ventricles in Ainsley's brain, designed to drain excess fluid, had stopped working. She was treated in Sydney before heading back to Wagga.

And that's the way it was: emergency, stress, a few laughs somehow, treatment and home.

Aaron remembers discussions about a potential new treatment said to be coming out later that year, a clinical trial that they were keen for Ainsley to participate in. So, with Ainsley home, although she had lost a little weight that year, things were positive.

The family of five then spent the spring school holidays on the south coast of New South Wales, as their eldest daughter prepared for her final term of kindergarten. The break was idyllic. The future would not be.

'She went back to school in October and that's when it happened,' Amanda says.

Autopsy Report (extract)

Dr Allan David CALA, 8 December 2014

Name: ***Ainsley Margaret DE JONG***

Post mortem no: ***141299***

Age: ***7 years (d.o.b. 07.12.06)***

Time & date of autopsy: 9am on 21st October 2014

AUTOPSY FINDINGS

POST MORTEM CHANGES:

The body *was cold to touch...*

MARKS or SCARS:

1. *A curved 150mm right sided craniotomy scar.*
2. *A curved 80mm right occipital craniotomy scar.*
3. *60mm scars below each breast.*

EVIDENCE OF MEDICAL INTERVENTION:

1. *An endotracheal tube exited the mouth.*
2. *An intravenous cannula in the right antecubital fossa.*
3. *An intravenous cannula in the left antecubital fossa.*

EVIDENCE OF INJURY:

1. *In the left upper parieto-occipital region of the head below the vertex was a collection of fine linear abrasions in an area 50mm diameter.*
2. *In the right upper forehead were three faint purple-red bruises in an area 25 × 15mm.*
3. *On the left shoulder was an area of yellowed abrasion 40mm diameter.*

CHAPTER 10

She's had enough, darl'

Fateful (adjective): *involving momentous consequences; decisively important*

Macquarie Concise Dictionary

MEMORIES CAN BECOME different things to different people, or can be clouded or confused with the passage of time and the workings of the brain. However, recollections of traumatic stress events seem to be stored differently; they are seared into the consciousness in a way the body can't forget.

Two parents will never be able to erase the events that unfolded on that fateful day in 2014.

Amanda says there's nothing blurry or uncertain about what she remembers of Friday, 17 October that year. Amanda was at home sick rather than at Coles, where she had taken a job after Audrey's arrival, for the ease of shorter shifts alongside running the family. She received a call from Willans Hill School. Something had happened to Ainsley.

'I was unwell that day, I was in bed,' she says. Amanda's best guess from the call she got was that Ainsley might need to go to hospital but she didn't imagine anything worse than possible minor injuries after a fall at school. Because she was sick, she asked Aaron to attend to it.

'Lynne [Aaron's mother] came and picked me up,' she says, 'and we caught up with the ambulance as it was going into the carpark of the hospital. I had no idea what we were going to face. All I thought was that she must've broken something. I didn't think – and they certainly didn't let on – that it was all that bad,' she says. 'Until I saw Aaron get out of the ambulance.'

Amanda knew panic when she saw it. Immediately, she felt it.

'They all just rushed. And I took off after her.'

~

Aaron's recall of the day is specific, and heart-wrenching.

'The last time I spoke with Ains she was in our bed with her two sisters the day before she died,' he says. 'I said goodbye to the girls and headed to work. They were laughing and mucking around together. Mum was picking Ains up from school that day and she was having a sleepover at her grandparents, as she normally did one night a week.'

Amanda rang him after lunch and said, '"Ains has had an accident at school," and she asked if I could go up there. I was busy at work and annoyed that Amanda couldn't go. I finished what I was doing before I left. I'm glad Amanda didn't have to witness what I saw when I got to the school, and I hate myself every day for the fact that I briefly put my work in front of everything.'

When he arrived, a staff member from the school office led him straight through the building and down a path.

'I could see some of the teachers holding up blankets as screens. Ains was lying face down on the concrete. I was trying to talk to her but she wasn't responding. Every few seconds she made a gurgling noise like she was gasping for air. I will never forget that noise, it still often wakes me up at night. I was on my knees trying to wake her up.'

The ambulance officer, who had started attending to her, looked up at Aaron and said, 'We gotta go.' He scooped her up and put her on a stretcher bed. Aaron was standing next to the bed and 'as he started pushing it quickly towards the ambulance, he told me to start pumping her chest. Walking alongside the bed, I did as I was instructed. "Harder and faster," he kept saying as I continued to pump her chest. When we got to the vehicle, another ambulance officer took over and I jumped over to the front seat.'

As they were heading to the hospital, the officer in the back was asking Aaron questions and 'basically verbalising what was happening to her. At the same time, Amanda was on the phone wanting to know what was going on, but I couldn't hear her through the blaring of the sirens. She was clearly getting frustrated, so I just told her to "Get to the hospital, ASAP!"'

Amanda met them there and 'Ains was taken into a room with all sorts of medical equipment and machines. There was a line on the floor that we were told to stay behind. Nurses were taking turns at the chest compressions and they were doing it very hard and fast … a lot harder and faster than I did. I often wonder if I was doing it well enough and if that might have changed things for her.'

People reassured Aaron that that wasn't the case, 'but the way I see it, they don't know. Sometimes I think it's just people saying what they think is the best thing for me to hear.'

For Aaron, 'the whole scenario was exactly like a scene from a movie … nurses everywhere, yelling out numbers and other stuff I didn't understand. By this time, all of our family had arrived and were watching. After a while, they started putting a tube down her throat.'

He saw two of Ainsley's front teeth knocked out with a metal part of the tube: 'I stopped them as they were doing it. They collected her teeth and kept going. Those teeth were the only teeth she had lost and we still have them.

'A little later, they tried to jumpstart her heart a couple of times, but it didn't work. It seemed like every time they stopped chest compressions, her heart would also stop. After what seemed like forever, the main doctor and another surgeon came over to tell us that they couldn't get Ains stable enough to take her upstairs and relieve the pressure in her brain.

'I eyeballed them,' Aaron says, 'and demanded that they "just fucking do it here".' He recalls there was a 'hopeless look in their eyes that gave me an overwhelming feeling. I looked at Amanda, who had tears in her eyes.'

'She's had enough, darl',' his wife said.

Aaron sensed that familiar sensation of a world going in slow motion.

'I couldn't hear a thing,' he says. 'The doctors and nurses started leaving the room. Amanda was sitting on a chair next to the bed and I was lying next to Ains on the other side. I had my head on her chest and there was a young nurse pumping the breathing apparatus. She had tears streaming down her face. The doctor came over and explained to her that Ains' "heart had stopped". As I listened to his words, I was overcome with that slow motion feeling I'd experienced moments prior. I remember my other two girls, Addison and Audrey, coming into the room. We cuddled Ains and talked to her.'

Reflection from Addi

Ainsley reminds me of a 2.0 version of Dora the Explorer, *who had a bobbed haircut and fringe just like her. Ains also had a little sidekick, her Dolly, like Dora had Boots, the blue monkey.*

Her big friendly smile would make anyone's day.

Things that made her happy were honey sandwiches, Tiny Teddies, Dolly and The Wiggles. *Ainsley always ate honey sandwiches with Tiny Teddies on the side; she couldn't go anywhere without her Dolly; and she enjoyed* The Wiggles *so much and would sing their songs by heart.*

Every time we are talking about her, it makes me smile as I think about all the memories we shared together. The happiness she made me feel comes back.

My favourite memory with my older sister is going to the beach in Batemans Bay. She would throw rocks and make sandcastles along the shore.

We had some great times at Omie's, where she would always put on a show for everyone to watch, whether it was dancing or singing. She always made people laugh.

Rainbows remind me of Ains. They remind me of her positive attitude towards her challenging life. After she was in a dark, sad hospital, she would always make everyone so happy with her bright smile. I think Ainsley would've handled her tumour and treatments so positively. I remember seeing Ainsley in her dark times and she wouldn't look like her happy self, but she would always try and not show it by cracking some funny jokes to the nurses or sending videos to Audrey and me back home.

There isn't a day that goes by when I don't think about her. I'll see things that remind me of her and I will just think to myself about Ainsley. I'll see things like her room on the way to school, pictures of her that pop up on my phone or hear songs on the radio.

Ainsley's death has completely changed me. If I get a great opportunity I think, like, 'If Ains had the choice, would she have done it?' If the answer is yes, then I will give it a crack! I try so hard to make Ainsley proud of me as she was my big sister and I hope she is looking down on me and thinking I'm doing a good job without her guiding the way.

Mum and Dad have said in the past that I had to really grow up, and while Ains was sick I had to be the older sister. But I really didn't realise that. I think it made me the responsible young person that I hope I am today.

Every day gets harder without her here with me, in the present, but it feels much better talking about her with others. That makes me feel like she's still alive and I have her with me in my heart.

There are heaps of songs that remind me of her. Once, when Ainsley had a school concert on, they sang the song 'Wishy Washy Washer Woman' and she yelled out to Omie in the audience. When I hear that song it always takes me back to that memory.

Another song Ains used to sing is 'That Power' and she would play it on her iPad and just dance and sing it.

Addison, Ainsley's little sister

CHAPTER 11

It felt like the hospital shut down

In the emergency ward on that unforgettable afternoon, Aaron remembers, amid the commotion, overhearing a nurse say Ainsley had been pushed, forcefully, by another student. While he and Amanda were waiting with Ainsley in a quiet room, police arrived. They moved to another room where, Aaron says, they were formally told that Ainsley had been pushed over by another child at school.

'I was in shock,' he says.

They didn't know it then, but this was the beginning of a new chapter of trauma – a long search for the comprehensive truth about what happened – kicking off right in the middle of the worst moment of their lives.

Aaron and Amanda were asked to leave so the nurses could take Ainsley through to the morgue. Aaron had no intention of leaving his daughter. Simply, but forcefully, he told them, 'I'm not going.'

'One of the hardest things to watch was the nurse just folding her up in a blue camping tarp and then the police putting her in a canvas bag and zipping it up. We walked along as they pushed Ains over to the morgue. We stayed a bit, said goodbye and went home.'

~

For Amanda, the next few days passed in a whirlwind of disbelief. She woke the following morning, wondering – desperately hoping, really – if it was a dream.

'I was just shaking my head going, "That didn't happen. Was that a nightmare?" It was very eerie,' she says.

It was a living nightmare, one from which they couldn't wake up. A Friday night that would have to be relived, over and over again. Amanda would often think of their extended family gathered in hope in a hospital emergency ward, only to witness a life slip away in front of their eyes.

'The whole family ended up in the room while they were trying to work on Ainsley,' she says. 'The nurses let us all stay there because everyone was so quiet. Nobody said anything. Nobody moved. Everyone was watching.

They were working on her and the doctor came over and said, "What do you want to do?" I said, "What do you mean what do we want to do?" He said, "Whichever way this ends, it isn't going to end well."'

The de Jongs were being warned that survival was unlikely, even if Ainsley was sustained by a tube and machine. Amanda remembers the moment of reality.

'They were doing all they could but you could feel maybe it was for us. There was a look like, "We would love to do more, but we can't." I just remember saying to Dr Pretty, "She's gone through enough. That's it." He motioned to the nurses, like, that's it. I went up close then and I remember the nurses. Some were crying. They were so down, so emotional. I remember thinking, this has really affected everyone. They were so beautiful. The whole hospital felt like it shut down. It just went dead quiet.'

The de Jongs were relieved to be in close contact with their other social worker, Michelle Knight. Married to one of Aaron's close friends, Michelle was an enormous help in a time of unimaginable horror.

'She was amazing,' Amanda says. 'She said, "Who do you want me to call?" And made sure all our family was able to be there. I remember Michelle saying the hospital were happy for everyone to stay there because they were dead-set quiet. Nobody moved. Nobody said anything.'

~

On Saturday morning, Amanda and Aaron returned to see Ainsley at the morgue.

'Due to the police investigation and impending autopsy,' Aaron says, 'we could only look at her through a glass screen. It was bloody tough. She still had the breathing tube in her mouth.' Her parents had two of her teeth.

Ainsley's body was to be transferred to Newcastle the next day, some 600 kilometres away, for an autopsy. The de Jongs were told it would take five days. Aaron didn't want her to be alone.

'I told them that I was going too,' he says. 'They looked at me like I was strange and denied my request. This didn't stop me from arguing back but it was all in vain. It might seem a bit unusual, but I just wanted to spend as much time as close to her as I could. I didn't give a shit if I was sleeping in my car in the carpark.'

~

The breaking in a human can be long and slow. Nothing prepares a parent for seeing their child lifeless and alone, and being unable to go to them.

'We weren't allowed to touch her,' Amanda says. 'We were allowed to sit with her that night she died. The hospital and the nurses were really good to us. But once we left and came back, the next day at the morgue, they said you've got to stay here and look at her from behind a glass window. I knew we weren't allowed to travel with her [to Newcastle] but it would've been nice to follow, to see it through. We weren't allowed to do anything, because of the coroner.'

Hard as it was, the de Jongs knew what was at stake. Protocols were in place to protect the integrity of the process. A child dies. An investigation follows. They would do their best to abide by the rules, because the rules were the road to explanations and answers. At least, that's what they understood.

From before Ainsley was born, right up to her death, life for the de Jongs had involved one shock after another. They rarely knew what was coming next, dealing only with each moment or emergency when it arrived. This time, at least, Ainsley's family thought they knew what would happen next: there'd be an autopsy, and then there'd be an inquest. Wouldn't there?

Autopsy Report (extract)

Dr Allan David CALA, 8 December 2014

Name: ***Ainsley Margaret DE JONG***
Post mortem no: ***141299***
Age: ***7 years (d.o.b. 07.12.06)***
Time & date of autopsy: 9am on 21st October 2014

CIRCUMSTANCES OF DEATH:

The information provided at the time of autopsy was taken from the police form P79a…

… During the lunch break on 17.10.14, Ainsley was in the playground and had been picking flowers. Another child pushed her to the upper chest region, causing her to fall backwards. The back of Ainsley's head struck a concrete surface. A teacher who had been present immediately went to her aid but by then, Ainsley was not moving.

Other staff were notified and Ainsley was attended to. At this time, Ainsley was unconscious and 'gulping' for air. An ambulance was called for, as was the child's father.

By the time [the] ambulance arrived, Ainsley's condition had deteriorated and she was pulseless. CPR was commenced and she was conveyed to Wagga Base Hospital. She was immediately attended to by doctors and was intubated. She had a cardiac arrest and was unable to be revived, with life pronounced extinct at 3.50pm.

A brain CT scan was able to be performed as part of resuscitation at the hospital. This showed the large pre-existent tumour with shunt in situ. *Scalp bleeding was present at the back of the head and there was acute subdural bleeding.*

CHAPTER 12

Ritual and procedure

According to its website, the Coroners Court of New South Wales is responsible for investigating sudden, unexpected and unnatural deaths in the state. The coronial jurisdiction is responsible for ordering a post-mortem or autopsy to deliver findings about a cause of death.

Coronial investigations review medical history, circumstances of death, the post-mortem, special reports from investigators and statements from witnesses. The coroner then reviews the evidence to determine whether an inquest is necessary. The court says it will also take into account the wishes of the family of the deceased person in reaching a decision; however, where the cause and manner of death are clear, proceedings can be finalised without an inquest.

Ainsley's cause of death was blunt trauma to the back of the head. Specifically, according to her autopsy report: 'BLUNT FORCE HEAD INJURY IN A CHILD WITH PILOCYTIC ASTROCYTOMA.'

Her parents do not believe her tumour was specifically a factor. As far as they understand, she was pushed, fell and died due to the force of her head hitting the ground.

Amanda says Ainsley's blood was low on platelets at the time. Her parents don't know whether a child without Ainsley's medical history might have had a better chance of surviving the blow to the head. But they expected to learn everything that led up to one specific, critical moment in time. They expected the coroner to examine in detail all of the circumstances behind a little girl going to school one day, and never coming home. So, the answers to their questions would wait. Now was a time for ritual again; a repeat of a process no parent wants to face once, let alone twice.

For the second time in just a few years, the de Jongs were helped by the Bance family as they prepared and then buried a child. At a time of extreme emotion and stress, small mercies arrive in a calming and compassionate presence.

'Scott, he was awesome,' Amanda says. 'You've got to be a special person to be a funeral director. I don't know how they do it. They are unbelievable, the most compassionate people. They were amazing.'

~

Around 300 people attended Ainsley de Jong's funeral at Sacred Heart Catholic Church in the Wagga Wagga suburb of Kooringal, including many children from Willans Hill School.

'A lot of the school went,' Amanda says. 'I remember one little girl coming up and saying, "Is Ainsley in heaven?" I thought, "Oh God." A lot of people didn't know how to react. But it was cute having the kids there.'

Carol Cattell read the eulogy on behalf of her Paediatric Outreach colleagues Sonia Wainwright, Diane Lawler and Carmel Brown, the rest of the staff at Wagga Base Hospital's Paediatric Department, and Ainsley's family.

Ainsley's resilience was acknowledged, from taking on the world without her twin brother to facing up to four long bouts of chemotherapy. Her first round was from four months of age until she was a little over a year-and-a-half; then, after two years of regular scans and blood tests, at three-and-a-half years of age for 12 months; at six years of age, a third round was given to counter the growth in her cerebral tumours; and, finally, in 2014, after a period of relative good health, Ainsley had commenced a fourth course. Her chemotherapy was always a careful juggle for medical staff, overseen by Professor Cohn, to rigorously balance providing effective treatment while maintaining Ainsley's quality of life.

Documenting a torturous medical journey illustrated Ainsley's inner strength and put into perspective the life she'd led. Because despite those ordeals, her nurses and family had been thrilled to see her growing into a confident young schoolgirl.

School was acknowledged as a big factor, with attendees hearing in Carol's eulogy that starting kindergarten at Willans Hill School in 2012 had been the making of Ainsley, helping her blossom and thrive, improving her communication skills and confidence, which in turn helped her cope with those ongoing treatments:

> Ainsley learnt colours at school and would be so proud to tell us she was holding a yellow lizard, a brown dinosaur, a pink pig or lastly a green soldier.
>
> She also learnt to count. She too was proud of her counting skills and there would be great cheering when she reached into the twenties and thirties.
>
> Her counting was utilised many times to get her through those difficult procedures.
>
> But Ainsley's greatest love was her music and dancing. The joy of dancing with Ainsley will stay vivid in all our minds, forever.

For Aaron, Ainsley's funeral is something of a blur. Much of her life he relives in vivid detail but her farewell is overshadowed by agony. He'd always been uneasy about Ainsley going to the cemetery to see Archie's grave; perhaps, he acknowledges, because he knew her time would come. But not now. And not like this.

He remembers his two girls and their cousins all looking down at Ainsley's coffin in the burial pit at the cemetery, before family and close friends adjourned to the home of Aaron's brother Nathan.

'I just wanted to go home,' Aaron says.

He couldn't say if he was hoping for peace. But peace wasn't looking for him.

PART 3

From Ainsley's Eulogy

Ainsley was very lucky to be surrounded by loving family. None more so than grandparents, Lynne and Arthur, affectionately called Omie and Op. You were such a reliable, amazing support for Ainsley, Aaron and Amanda. Thank you both for your support in these difficult and demanding years, and for loving Ainsley. It was obvious Ainsley adored you both and we know that love was mutual.

To all the doting aunts, uncles and friends, we thank you from the bottom of our hearts and appreciate all you did for our family.

A special thank you to all of Ainsley's cousins. You were so loving and caring with Ainsley. It was beautiful to watch you all be so gentle with her and it was very obvious that she loved you coming to visit her in hospital.

Aaron and Amanda, what devoted parents you are. You were patient when you needed to be and so resilient when faced with many challenging times. You were supportive in every way, especially during Ainsley's treatments. Having you there to help, particularly when Ainsley was upset, was so greatly appreciated. Your ability to find humour in the most difficult situations was amazing. We often would find ourselves laughing over trivial things, I guess making it easier for everyone.

You should be truly proud of yourselves for the strength and tenacity you showed whilst caring for Ainsley, and we know your love for her was immeasurable.

Carol Cattell, Paediatric Outreach Nurse, Wagga Wagga Base Hospital
Sacred Heart Church, October 2014

CHAPTER 13

No one seems to care

LIFE WITHOUT AINSLEY was always going to be difficult. But it wasn't meant to be this hard.

Her death had come completely against the rhythm of her life at that time. A family that had grown used to medical emergencies and hospitals – a family well-versed in hard-to-have discussions – wasn't ready for a chance encounter to snatch her away.

'We knew she was going to die one day but it wasn't going to be then – she was going well. Things were happening, it was all going okay,' Aaron says.

Police had visited the de Jongs at home the day after Ainsley's death and informed them that no charges would be laid against the schoolgirl who had pushed their daughter. Neither Amanda nor Aaron was looking for a student to be charged. They did, however, expect a full and thorough investigation.

'We wanted to know everything that happened and to prevent it from ever happening again,' Amanda says. 'We sent her to Willans Hill School because we thought she was going to be safe.'

A detective was assigned to the case and, Aaron says, it was communicated that the inquest wouldn't happen until the police paperwork had been completed.

That took far longer than they'd hoped.

'Months went past and late one night the detective called me and asked me to come down to the police station,' Aaron says. 'He then broke down in tears and told me he hadn't done the paperwork. The case had brought up issues for him from another case years earlier. I felt sorry for him but I was also frustrated.'

In the meantime, the school was in contact with the grieving parents a couple of times. Both were bizarre conversations in the circumstances, according to the de Jongs.

'I got a phone call from the school two days after Ainsley had passed,' Amanda says, 'asking me if I was going to sue the child's mum and dad, because they'd heard rumours. "No! Why would I do that?" was my immediate reaction. I look back now and I'm so angry about the way that I was … I was too nice. I said, "Of course not", and they said they were just checking.

'That was one phone call, and then I got another one when we went away after the funeral, just to get away. They basically called to offer us a $15,000 shut-up fee, really.'

The family was on the road, heading north for a break in the hope they could somehow take the first steps in putting a life back together again. On their way out of Wagga Wagga, Amanda took that second call, which immediately set alarm bells ringing for them.

'They said they'd been contacted by the department [of education] and they wanted our family to have the money, that our beautiful family deserved that,' Amanda says. 'The way they spoke to me, I knew something was up.'

Amanda asked Aaron to pull over, and they discussed it, right there on the side of the highway.

'The explanation was that the $15,000 would help out with things such as the funeral,' Aaron says. 'We were told that they needed us to come into the school and sign a form so the funds could be released. After what we'd been through, who would have thought there'd be a catch? It was like throwing a red rag at a bull for the both of us. I rang a solicitor friend of mine and she instructed us not to do anything. When we got back, she put us in touch with another solicitor by the name of John Potter.'

That phone call offering financial assistance, on the proviso of signing some forms – and, potentially, signing away some of their rights at the most vulnerable time in their lives – remains a source of contempt for the de Jongs. They weren't thinking of legal action or ramifications. Emotional support was what they needed then. But the system was already anticipating a legal battle and preparing its defence.

'That's a lot of money for a family,' Amanda says.

But to her, it immediately felt like dirty money; an offer to make them complicit in ensuring everything was neatly locked away, and that there'd never be any further questions about what happened that spring afternoon at Willans Hill School.

The de Jongs were not going to give up their right to ask questions and pursue the truth. Amanda says they were lucky to be in a position to consider their options, and to be able to say no to what they felt would amount to hush money.

'I just think, "You arseholes!" Another family might have had to just take that and give up their right to find out more later. It's disgusting really,' Amanda says. 'I've got a lot of hurt with that school. I just feel so …'

Words almost fail her.

'I felt like it was swept under the carpet because it was at a special school. If that had happened at another primary school, I think everyone would've heard all about it.'

Amanda harbours a broken-hearted disappointment, rather than bitter resentment.

'We did everything right by them. We always paid our school fees there, and those sorts of things,' she says. 'Then to get told no one's allowed to contact you. And to be treated like we're … like we're the ones in the wrong …'

At the time of Ainsley's death, Aaron and Amanda thought the school shared their sorrow and would be a source of support. Aaron recalls how the week after Ainsley died, Amanda visited the school, taking flowers to the office and thanking the staff for everything they had done for Ains.

'Little did we know,' he says, 'the school had already had a staff meeting and all staff were told not to make contact or talk to us in any way. This hurt. To be honest it pissed me right off. All we ever heard from the school was a call offering us money not to sue them. That's it and nothing since. Even after we ended up going through the civil case, they went out of their way to be unhelpful.

'I keep trying to be empathetic and put myself in the position of the staff but it still disappoints me that there was only one teacher's aide that stood up for what they knew to be right. She left the school after Ains died and made a point of seeing us. She showed a sense of compassion towards us and for this, we are very grateful.'

Autopsy Report (extract)

Dr Allan David CALA, 8 December 2014

Name:	***Ainsley Margaret DE JONG***
Post mortem no:	***141299***
Age:	***7 years (d.o.b. 07.12.06)***
Time & date of autopsy:	***9am on 21st October 2014***

OPINION

Based on what I have observed, my experience and training, and the information supplied to me:

Ainsley Margaret De Jong died on 17th October 2014 at Wagga Base Hospital and that the cause of death is as follows:

1. DIRECT CAUSE:

Disease or condition leading to death:

(a) BLUNT FORCE HEAD INJURY IN A CHILD WITH PILOCYTIC ASTROCYTOMA

ANTECEDENT CAUSES:

Morbid conditions, if any, giving rise to the above cause, stating the underlying condition last:

*(b) *******

*(c) *******

2. Other significant conditions contributing to the death but not relating to the disease or condition causing it:

CIRCUMSTANCES OF DEATH:

...

COMMENTS:

1. *An external examination in the presence of Crime Scene police and brain CT scan were performed.*
2. *An irregularly shaped area of abrasion was in the upper left parieto-occipital region near the vertex of the scalp (top of head), under which was scalp bruising.*

3. *There was fresh bleeding around the brain on CT scan. The base of the brain was abnormal with a large tumour evident in the region of the hypothalamus.*
4. *It seems likely the child sustained severe head impact trauma when she landed on a hard concreted surface. This appears to have caused a sudden but severe 'jolt' to the brain resulting in almost immediate loss of consciousness and cardiac arrest soon after.*
5. *Discussions were held with family members and coroners from Wagga and Sydney. Ultimately it was decided that a* post mortem *CT brain scan and external examination of the body were to be performed, and any further (invasive) procedure was not indicated under the circumstances.*

CHAPTER 14

Nature of injury: fatality

> One student (special needs student) slapped another student (also special needs student) and the student was removed from the playground.
>
> The student that was slapped was crying/upset and the teacher said she could have some quiet time in the classroom.
>
> The student was then taken off the playground / escorted to the classroom by the teacher.
>
> As the student and teacher were approaching the classroom (approx 5–6m away), the student pushed another student (student has a fragile skull) whom fell over and her head struck the ground (concrete) and was immediately unconscious.
>
> An ambulance was then called to the school.

Five sentences in a NSW Department of Education and Training Incident Report Form, completed by the teacher on duty, 'Witness (1 of 1)', offer a raw description of the event that ended the life of Ainsley Margaret de Jong, aged seven, at a Wagga Wagga school one Friday afternoon in 2014.

The incident report was entered on 20 October, three days after Ainsley's death. It's not until page three of the four-page form that the seriousness of the matter is understood:

Nature of Injury/Illness:	Fatality
Bodily Location of Injury/Illness:	Head (other than eye, ear and face)
Side of Body:	Not applicable
Mechanism of Injury/Illness:	Accidental (assault)
Agency of Injury/Illness:	Human Agencies

There's no underestimating the enormity of a child dying in a school playground. The Incident Report Form was far from the only record of Ainsley's death within the department. A similar, albeit more basic, account of events was entered in a Safety and Security Directorate Report, also completed on Monday 20 October, at 9.36 am. But the first official account of what happened on 17 October was being compiled immediately on the Friday afternoon in order to be sent up the chain of command as soon as possible, as a formal brief.

Ainsley was part of a community, with friends at school, and under teachers who'd taken a keen interest in her, staff who had taken her a long way in terms of development and confidence.

Her sudden death on the grounds of Willans Hill School *was* a big deal. And, in the immediate aftermath, the de Jongs felt they shared their deep sense of loss with the school and could draw strength from their community.

This place where their daughter had been cared for, where they'd seen she was learning, growing in confidence, and growing up into the world, had also suffered a massive shock and been sent into a state of tumult. The series of tremors it set off in the broader education system was revealed when the de Jongs successfully sought access to files under the *Government Information (Public Access) Act 2009* ('GIPA Act') more than two years later.

Among 199 pages of records identified as relevant to their application in early 2017 are timelines and chronologies detailing what happened and when in the minutes, hours and days following the incident involving Ainsley on Friday, 17 October 2014:

> At approximately 1.50pm, during the school's lunch break, a student with autism became aggressive and was removed from the playground in accordance with the school's procedure. This caused another student … to become stressed and aggressive. [She] lashed out and pushed Ainsley to the ground. Ainsley hit her head on the ground and lost consciousness.

Fourteen lines down – one hour and 40 minutes later in real time – the fatality is recorded: '*Ainsley died at approximately 3.30pm.*'

Between 1.50 pm and 1.55 pm, an ambulance had been called to Willans Hill School.

At 2 pm, the de Jongs were called and informed of an accident.

Sometime between 2 pm and 2.30 pm, Ainsley was transported to Wagga Wagga Base Hospital.

A counsellor was at the school at 2.30 pm.

The school principal, Chris Lennon, was on leave at the time, but was called at 2.36 pm by the school administrative manager. Her three assistant principals were each in charge of one area of the school.

At 2.45 pm a call was made to the Wagga Wagga office of the education department, who then alerted the region's relieving director of Public Schools NSW, Anne Nolan.

At 4.25 pm police attended the school.

At 4.39 pm, teacher's aide Suzy Lawler, who had followed Aaron, Ainsley and the ambulance to the hospital, informed the school of the death of one of their students. An assistant principal informed the staff.

At 4.44 pm, Public Schools NSW acting director at the Wagga office, Jim Roworth, was contacted by the principal and at 4.47 pm, Ms Nolan was notified.

The department's media unit was informed at 4.50 pm, while Ms Nolan contacted Ms Lennon to offer support at

4.50 pm, shortly before the principal arrived at the school at 5 pm.

At 5.02 pm, relieving executive director Public Schools NSW, Graham Kahabka, was informed and minutes later information was provided to him and Bob Aston, the director of education services, for the pair to prepare a briefing paper for the deputy secretary of the Department of Education and Communities, Greg Prior.

At 5.50 pm, Ms Lennon attempted to call the de Jongs, and also began ringing parents from the school community.

This was a major operation underway, involving the school, the department and police, and reaching the state government.

At 6 pm, a counsellor was organised to be at the school on Monday, and various support programs and resources were explored for teachers and students. The timeline notes that assistant principal Janelle Urbanivicius returned to the school at 6 pm from her home nearly 50 kilometres away, and visited the Wagga Wagga police station at 6.20 pm to provide a statement.

By 6.10 pm, the department's school safety and response unit and its work health and safety directorate had apparently been contacted.

At 7.45 pm the brief from Aston and Kahabka was emailed out, providing a basic description of the events of the afternoon, the outcome, and the plans for follow-up.

At 7.49 pm, the director of the safety and security directorate provided advice to the departmental directors of media and workplace health and safety, as well as to the legal services directorate and to a seconded police officer who led the school safety and response unit.

At 9.35 am the following morning, the timeline reports, Mr Kahabka rang Mr Aaron de Jong and left a message of sympathy, offering any support available.

~

Throughout Saturday, plans were being prepared for staff assistance at the school on Monday. By Saturday afternoon, the NSW Department of Education and Communities' legal services directorate had already raised the possibility of sourcing financial assistance for the de Jongs to assist with funeral costs. It's referred to in a 5.34 pm email that noted staff responsible for managing civil litigation claims had been notified and would seek to source funds.

When school resumed the following week, the department's timeline says, the principal 'held a staff meeting to start the day and inform staff of the support available to students and staff, and her expectations re professionalism and safety'; three counsellors were on site along with three additional casual teaching staff; a workplace health and safety incident report was logged; the 'reporting accidents at school' documentation was completed; legal services offered support to any staff required to give statements; and arrangements for the funeral were discussed, in terms of what it would mean at the school. Under the time frame of 'Ongoing support', the department's chronology says information likely to be required by the coroner was gathered, copied and stored securely. It says witness statements were checked by the principal for accuracy and fact. It records that there was 'very positive contact from the de Jong family with Chris Lennon'.

The released documents don't state that staff were told whether they could be in contact with the family; there are no minutes or details as to what was discussed in staff meetings, or a written record of the instructions or advice given.

The $15,000 offer for the de Jongs, made available by the Department of Education and Communities to assist with funeral expenses, is confirmed. But it's a curious situation. There's the mention of funds being sought the day after Ainsley's death. The timeline provided to WorkCover says the offer was later discussed by Anne Nolan and Chris Lennon on 3 November. The records say Ms Lennon decided it would be appropriate for her to contact the family, and that she will inform Anne Nolan of the outcome. That was the phone call the de Jongs received on their way out of Wagga Wagga for a family break as they were trying to come to terms with Ainsley's death;

a phone call that sparked suspicion about what exactly was being offered.

However, neither the outcome of those discussions with the de Jongs nor any follow-up at all about the matter is ever mentioned again in any of the documents released to the family. It's as though they should believe that no one in the state bureaucracy ever found out if the money was accepted or required, let alone asked as to why or why not. There's no minute or email or document stating if the $15,000 was accepted and paid, or declined and no longer required.

The list of events and actions mentioned above are only a snapshot of a comprehensive, intricately detailed chronology of events – a document among dozens and dozens of pages of other correspondence relating to Ainsley. It seems unusual that funding could be explored within 24 hours of Ainsley's death, that $15,000 was then sourced, an offer to the family is documented as ready to be made, and then the matter is never referred to again. It's close to unbelievable.

One legal mind warned the de Jongs at the time: 'That phone call to you will never have happened.'

~

The family was burying a child, trying to cope with the trauma and make out what life would look like next.

Meanwhile, inside the machine of government bureaucracy, the wheels were turning quickly from the outset, seemingly with a focus on avoiding legal action.

As early as 21 November 2014, an email from Peter McGhee, Senior Legal Officer, Department of Education and Communities, notes that he has 'opened a claim in this matter as I was anticipating that Ainsley's parents may litigate down the track. I was able to secure our self to pay up to $15,000 to pay for the funeral and family counselling expenses as an ex gratia payment.'

That's the $15,000 the de Jongs didn't take up at a meeting they never attended after being told they'd have to sign some paperwork as a condition of its release. That's the $15,000 offer that disappears and is never mentioned again in the cache of paperwork – emails, notes, letters, forms, documents – released to Ainsley's family, a file they were told contains all the information held by the department relating to her death at school.

~

Aaron had submitted his application at the beginning of February 2017, seeking access to 'Information on the investigation into the death of my daughter Ainsley de Jong at Willans Hill School on 17 October 2014'. A month later, a Principal Information Access Officer at the Information Access Unit advised Aaron in a formal seven-page letter that his request was successful 'in part' and set out legal justifications for and against the release of some information.

Nearly 200 pages of NSW Department of Education records and paperwork were identified as relevant to the application after a search of electronic records (shared drives and document management systems), physical files (hard copies) and individuals' email accounts. Twenty-five pages came from the legal services directorate, 44 pages from the health and safety directorate, and the last 130 pages of records were obtained from Willans Hill School.

The Information Access Officer advised that some sections of some pages were redacted because they contained personal information of third parties, or were considered not to be relevant or within the scope of the application. Pages 134 to 199 were withheld entirely because they contained personal and health information of other students.

Many pages were copies of Ainsley's medical history and medical reports, prior to her enrolment at the school, including details of her personal plan at Willans Hill, emergency contacts, her care profile, mealtime procedures, medication and behaviour support plans.

There's a draft response to the WorkCover investigation opened in the weeks following Ainsley's death. A series of 13 questions sent to the Department of Education and Communities' work health and safety directorate on 21 November 2014 were answered with input and advice from the NSW Crown Solicitor's Office. The enquiries asked for information including:

- details of witnesses [one to the altercation, 12 staff involved in the response to the altercation]
- information on Ainsley's health provided prior to her starting school
- systems and risk management plans in place for students, in particular for Ainsley given her health history
- procedures in place for managing violence and aggression in a special needs school
- whether Ainsley and the other student involved had any history of altercations [no]
- the ratio of staff to students in the classroom and on the playground [one to eight in class and in the junior playground on the day]
- whether any procedures or systems had been modified as a result of the incident.

The school said its playground monitoring and behaviour risk management had 'been reviewed but no modification has been identified as necessary'.

The detailed chronology of events was supplied by the department, and the school's response also noted that 'Willans Hill School Principal Chris Lennon is in continuous communication with the parents of the deceased …'

The finalised answers were sent to WorkCover on 2 December 2014. Later emails confirm the WorkCover investigation was closed in February 2015.

~

On 21 October, four days after Ainsley's death, and the same day her autopsy was being conducted in Newcastle, Anne Nolan, relieving director at Public Schools New South Wales, let colleagues know in an email:

> The family contacted the principal and were nothing less than inspirational in their praise for the school. The mother has also met with the teacher and aide who were on the spot at the time and indicated that they had valued everything the school had done for Ainsley.

The de Jongs *were* thankful for all the school had done for Ainsley when she was alive, and happy and hopeful of ongoing community support after her death. They indicated that they were happy for any staff, students and families to attend Ainsley's funeral, which was coming up on Monday, 27 October. The breakdown in the relationship came later, after Ainsley's death appeared to be reduced to a 'conditional offer' they could take or leave. Perhaps more damaging and hurtful though was the discovery that teachers and staff at the school had been instructed not to have any further contact with the de Jong family.

~

Society runs on the back of systems, organisations, bureaucracies, processes and procedures. But what happens when the structures that are supposed to help communities become more important than the people they are meant to serve?

How can a human life – a laughing, smiling, *giving* little life of almost eight years – be so swiftly swept up in the apparatus and operations of government?

Ainsley de Jong could dance – she could dance, she could sing, she could laugh. She was strong and resilient. She made pity redundant by inspiring others instead. Yet, in the paper trail after Ainsley's death at school, it wasn't long before she became a series of reference numbers in the subject line of emails in the government system, as a legal process swung into action.

On Tuesday afternoon, 28 October 2014 – the day after her funeral – an email was sent from the NSW Crown Solicitor's office to a Suncorp 'Claims Advisor TMF (Treasury Managed Fund) Health and DEC (Department of Education and Communities) Liability Claims', referring to:

> Subject: MPL2210822 – De Jong A v State of New South Wales – Incident at Willans Hill SSP (CSO Ref. 201402762) – Matter Program

In others, the tragedy of the student killed at school is a series of three reference codes:

> Subject: De Jong MPL2210822 DEC ref LEGAL14/1589 CSO ref 201402762

More than a year later, in November 2015, a similar reference is the subject line of an email from Suncorp's Amanda Karamihalis, now 'Senior Claims Officer, TMF Claims, Client Management Services'. Ms Karamihalis asks Lucy Pinnock from the NSW Crown Solicitor's Office and Peter McGhee from the Department of Education whether the police investigation into Ainsley's death has been finalised, and if there's been 'any contact from the family or legal representative or notification from the Coroner concerning a possible inquest?'

The remainder of the email is removed, replaced only by a code indicating it was 'not relevant' to Aaron's request for information relating to the death of his daughter. It's difficult not to wonder what else was included in that email – an email specifically related to Ainsley de Jong's death – and wonder how it is not relevant to Ainsley's death.

In the 133 pages of information released to the de Jongs, there's no record of a reply to this email.

There are pages of emails planning and discussing the department's response to the WorkCover investigation.

There are email trails and questions seeking to ascertain exactly who informed who, and how, in the work health and safety directorate on the Friday evening, because the forms weren't completed until Monday, creating concerns of a possible breach of the legal requirement to inform WorkCover within 24 hours.

There are records of the 'Reporting Accidents at School' documentation being completed with witnesses providing their statements with the support of a staff member and a counsellor.

Pages 71 to 75 of the documents released to the de Jongs contain a lengthy statement from the then-principal at Willans Hill School, Chris Lennon. Dated 12 November 2014, the document gives an overview of staffing, procedures for the school's three learning teams (senior, middle and junior), as well as individual plans specific to each student. All 70 students had personalised learning and support plans, including behaviour and personal care procedures for students with those needs.

The statement said three teachers were responsible for 34 students in the high-school playground, 20 students from the primary and high school sections usually attended the library at lunchtime, and two teachers looked after eight students each in the junior playground. It notes staff at Willans Hill School were trained in emergency care in 2013, and were well aware of, and had access to, the school's emergency management plan: 'In some periods we have had to call 000 on a weekly or even more frequent basis.'

Regarding Ainsley, Chris Lennon said her moderate intellectual disability (due to her brain tumour) and autism diagnosis had made her eligible for placement at the school. She said staff were well aware of Ainsley's shunt, and the seriousness of any head injuries. The principal said the school had also monitored Ainsley's health through her bouts of chemotherapy treatment and its side effects, and encouraged the whole school community to remember Ainsley's vulnerability when considering whether children were well enough to come to school.

She believed Ainsley loved school and all of the activities: 'We were delighted with her progress. Delighted with her.'

After paragraphs relating to other students, Ms Lennon's statement concludes that, while she was away at the time, she was confident staff followed the plans in place and said she was proud of every one of them:

> I believe that this was a terrible accident. I am working hard to ensure that my staff and my school community can heal from this harrowing experience. Our school has an excellent reputation based on quality education programs and an excellent individual approach to students and their needs. Our school community has been overwhelming in their support of my staff and our programs, during this heart-breaking time.

Reflection from Carol

I think of Ainsley every day as I have a Dolly pillow on my bed. (Lynne gave it to me, for which I am forever grateful.) So Ainsley's memory will live on forever.

Dolly made Ainsley happy. Dancing and music made her happy. I often do think she was most happy when her treatment was finished and she was frantically waving and singing out goodbye to everyone, and walking out the door to go home.

I often think of Ainsley when we discuss brain tumour patients and are chatting with the Sydney nurses.

I will never forget that day in the emergency room. It made me realise that – chronically unwell or not – events can happen to anyone and cut short their precious life, so unexpectedly. I try to encourage families to enjoy their little children as much as possible.

I feel Ainsley's life was cut short, there is no doubt about that. How long she had to live because of her brain tumours, who knows? I just wish her family could have had the time to deal with that possibility over a good length of time, not in 45 minutes.

Ainsley loved Thomas the Tank Engine *and I do think of her when I see that on TV. My name badge was a* Thomas the Tank Engine *badge. She was so cute, when she saw it on my shirt she would point and say 'Thomas' and then laugh.*

I gave my Thomas the Tank Engine *name badge to Amanda. She put it in the coffin with Ainsley. Hopefully she held that and thought of us at the hospital sometimes.*

Carol Cattell, Wagga Paediatric Outreach Nurse

CHAPTER 15

Nothing felt right

AINSLEY DE JONG'S DEATH changed Suzy Lawler. It changed her life, her sense of perspective and her understanding of the way things work. It challenged her view of the world. But it wouldn't change her values.

Suzy is the sole staff member who, Aaron said, 'stood up for what they knew to be right' and showed a compassion towards the de Jongs for which they'll be forever grateful.

~

'I worked at Willans Hill as a teacher's aide for approximately five or six years and I loved every minute of it,' Suzy says. 'I loved the students, I loved feeling like I was helping and making a difference with their lives. It was a privilege to watch them grow and learn and build confidence to take on the world, however that might be.'

Suzy was on staff, albeit working with the senior students, when Ainsley first went to school. And she was by Ainsley's side in the playground on what would be the seven-year-old's last day – using her jacket to shield the eyes of her favourite little student – and fearing the worst as everyone sweated on the arrival of an ambulance.

'I feel like I remember everything from that fateful Friday – although I've tried very, very hard to forget it all,' she says. 'I'm really struggling with putting that day into words … I just remember chaos. It was your worst nightmare. It felt like the ambulance took forever – they probably didn't at all, but everything felt like it was going in slow motion. She was just lifeless. You know when you just know that this is not … this is not a normal fall. I just knew we needed help. We desperately needed help.'

The tragedy will stay with Suzy forever.

Simply meeting Ainsley years earlier had been life-changing too. Life-affirming, really, coming across a little girl who was such a force of nature.

'When I think of Ains, I automatically smile. Just thinking of her brings me happiness,' she says. 'I remember thinking how lucky I was when she started at Willans Hill as I got to see her! She was unbelievably cute, so tiny, and knew what she wanted. She definitely was adorable and she caught everybody's eye … if there was going to be a pin-up girl, it would've been her! She was full of spunk. Full of character. She was her own person. There was no messing with her.

'Some mornings, she could put it on – as all kids do – for her parents. Sometimes it was an effort to get her into the school gates or an effort to get her out of the car. She was that little one that would, you know, go stiff in the car seat and not move.'

Suzy remembers Ainsley's 'pyjama stage', a period when her bold personality was emerging and the little student would refuse to get dressed at home.

'Right or wrong, Amanda wasn't going to be able to get her into her uniform for school. She'd turn up in her pyjamas!' Suzy says. 'The principal would talk to her and she'd be off into the office and next minute come out happily in her little school uniform … not an ounce of trouble at school. It was like, yeah, I've upset my family so now I'll walk in, put my clothes on happily, and go about my day.'

Suzy laughs regularly – almost subconsciously – talking about Ainsley.

'She just had something about her, this spunk, that made sure you were drawn to her. She stood out, but not in a bad way … For all the trouble that must've been happening around her – her health and everything – she was always just a happy little thing. I'm very confident in saying she stole everyone's heart and it was easy to see why.'

When she was on playground duty, bus duty or simply passing through the school, Suzy delighted in coming across Ainsley, often dancing to her favourite music.

'She was this little doll. She was tiny. It was the highlight of the day to see Ains in the playground. She was always happy, always had a smile. She'd have her Dolly with her,' she says. 'I remember her confidence and her character growing. I wasn't working in her room but from what I would hear and what I could see, she was going ahead in leaps and bounds, just flourishing.'

Wagga Wagga is a city but it's not *that* big. Suzy knew of Ainsley before she was born, having shared antenatal classes with the de Jongs when Amanda was pregnant with twins. In fact, when Suzy went to hospital to give birth to her first child, Archer, she came across Aaron and Amanda there at the same time.

'We made the terrible mistake of thinking they were there having the twins but that was when they found out that Archie was no longer,' she says. The occasion cemented an association that ensured Suzy would always be acutely aware of the random and sometimes unforgiving nature of life's journey.

'We had Archer, they had Archie … it was just all so close.'

Coincidentally, Suzy also formed a close friendship with Aaron's sister, Emma, over the years.

'Emma and I have become really great friends – my kids actually call her Aunty Em – and she would sometimes bring Ainsley to school for drop-offs. It was a whole family affair with little Ains,' Suzy says.

On the day that Ainsley died, Suzy had been in contact with Emma during the day, saying they'd see each other after school because 'Aunty Em' was coming to pick up her niece, given Amanda was at home in bed sick. So, Ainsley was already on her mind, even before a student came in at lunchtime carrying a card indicating a teacher needed assistance.

'We had little signs that students could carry to the staff room if one of the teachers on playground duty needed help. Usually it was something little, like a student needed help to go to the toilet or something,' Suzy says. 'I remember the student was Tristan, one of our senior boys and a very capable boy. I remember him being quite vocal and I heard the name "Ainsley". Knowing Ains, I ran out the back and it's just … the rest is … I don't know.

'I remember her lying there on the cement and I took off my denim jacket because the sun was shining on her little face and I wanted to shield her from the sun. I don't know if it was five minutes or two hours – there was no sense of time – but I remember it being chaotic. I remember Aaron arriving at the school and that was pretty daunting. He arrived around the same time as the paramedics and he was – understandably – a mess. There was this high-pitched screaming and yelling, begging Ainsley, like "stick with me".'

Next was the rush to the hospital. Suzy followed the ambulance, calling Emma and telling her to 'get your parents and get to the hospital'. She felt a small tug of war playing out in her head and in her gut, trying to convey the urgency and seriousness of the situation, all the while not wanting to spark a full panic, hoping things wouldn't be as bad as they appeared.

The de Jongs' extended family converged on Wagga Base Hospital, including Ainsley's little sisters, Addison and Audrey. Suzy took them to her own parents' place nearby, hoping to offer a distraction by playing with their pets, including guinea pigs. It was a short detour.

'It wasn't long before we had a call from the hospital that the girls needed to come back … to say goodbye.'

The girls returned with Suzy.

'I remember walking in and thinking, this is every person's worst nightmare.'

It wasn't a scene that needed any drumming home, but Suzy knew Dr Pretty – he had looked after her own children, and here he was trying to help in the final stages of Ainsley's short life. That rocked her. And she could see that everyone in the room, from hospital staff to family, were distraught, in the grip of a painful tragedy.

'It touched everyone. It was kind of like a movie scene but worse,' she says. 'It was really confronting. Just seeing … and hearing the sounds of everyone. It was heart-wrenching.'

As the reality settled on those in attendance, that Ainsley's brief but powerful life was over, Suzy realised it was her task to call the school.

'I can't remember who I told the news to. I think I told them, "She didn't make it." I don't even remember telling the school I was leaving. I don't think I did. I think I just felt like this is a proper emergency. These people are going to need help. I stayed at the hospital for quite a while. Amanda's brother and sister-in-law and kids turned up. People were arriving. I sort of sat out the front of the hospital and was telling people to go on in, the family was waiting.'

Amid all that was swirling around her, Suzy remembered that her own five kids would be at their school, waiting for her.

'I forgot about my own children. Far out, my own kids! They were only little … I rang my dad. He says he just knew I was beside myself and understood there was an accident and he went and picked them up for me.'

~

The weekend passed in a blur, with Suzy among those to descend on the de Jong family home, visiting to pass on condolences, help stock the fridge and freezer, and generally do whatever they thought might be useful.

As the weekend wore on, the teacher's aide was almost looking forward to returning to school – to a support network, where the community would throw its arms around a family that needed help, not to mention each other. But even eight years after Ainsley's death, the question of what it felt like at work – where teachers had lost a student and students had lost a classmate – almost numbs Suzy Lawler.

'Umm … it really threw me,' she says. 'The weekend was full of disbelief and such awfulness. But I thought, 'Well, I'll go into work on the Monday because school communities pull together." I remember thinking, "This is going to be really good because that's what schools do, get around families, help them, help each other … you pull together and you talk about it." I was thinking we'd be talking about "let's do this" or "let's do that" [for the de Jongs]. But it was very matter of fact. It was kind of like, "This happened on the Friday. We don't talk about it. No one is to be in touch with the family."'

The word shocked doesn't do justice to Suzy's reaction. She'd been at the hospital when a student passed away just three days earlier, and at the family's house since as part of a wider support network helping friends in need.

'I said, "I've already been there. I spent the weekend there", and they were like, "Well, you don't go back."'

It still staggers the former staff member.

'I was fixated on sending flowers. I remember saying we need to send flowers and was told, "We don't want to send flowers; we don't want to be seen as showing we're guilty of anything."'

Suzy thinks, in the end, flowers were sent. But there was no mistaking the tone and feeling of how things were going to roll for staff at the school. In what seems a critical failure of leadership, a sense of defensiveness and concern about the investigations to come – one which may have been understandable elsewhere in the corridors of power and responsibility within the Department of Education, perhaps – had somehow filtered all the way down and infiltrated a school community dealing with a fatality. Worse yet, it dictated the response.

'I remember thinking, "Who's guilty? What are we even talking about? There's someone burying a child. Can't we just send flowers?"' Suzy says. 'I didn't expect it to be like that. I thought we'd just wrap our arms around the de Jongs. I wasn't even thinking about how it had happened. I thought it was a tragic accident. I still believe it was a tragic accident. But I think it could've been dealt with a lot better afterwards. Regardless of what happened, you just surround them with love.'

~

The Polish novelist Olga Tokarczuk won the Nobel Prize for Literature in 2018. In her Nobel Lecture acceptance speech, the trained psychologist spoke about an important form of love:

> Tenderness is the most modest form of love. It is the kind of love that does not appear in the scriptures or the gospels, no one swears by it, no one cites it. It has no special emblems or symbols, nor does it lead to crime, or prompt envy.
>
> It appears wherever we take a close and careful look at another being, at something that is not our 'self'.
>
> Tenderness is spontaneous and disinterested; it goes far beyond empathetic fellow feeling. Instead it is the conscious, though perhaps slightly melancholy, common sharing of fate. Tenderness is deep emotional concern about another being, its fragility, its unique nature, and its lack of immunity to suffering and the effects of time. Tenderness perceives the bonds that connect us, the similarities and the sameness between us. It is a way of looking that shows the world as being alive, living, interconnected, cooperating with, and codependent on, itself.
>
> © The Nobel Foundation 2018

Whether she expressed it or not – whether she knew it or not – tenderness was at the heart of Suzy Lawler's reactions and response in October 2014, and ever since.

But it appears to have been missing from the formal actions of her employer, the NSW Department of Education, in the wake of Ainsley's death on school grounds.

~

It would take years for Suzy to even begin to process what she witnessed on that Friday afternoon at work, what happened to a little girl whose extended family she'd come to know well.

'Leaving the school with Ainsley on a stretcher and Aaron with just this primal scream coming out of him … willing her to be okay … I used to close my eyes at night and that was all I could hear,' she says. 'I would think, "Why?" You wouldn't wish it upon anybody. But I just think, "My Lord … why did it have to be Ainsley?"'

Three days after they'd lost a primary school student on the playground, Suzy expected the school's top two priorities would be working out ways to support Ainsley's family and checking on the welfare of students and staff.

'When I turned up on the Monday I was thinking, this is affecting all of us. It didn't matter what team you worked in or whatever … a little girl has just tragically died in our school community and it's affecting everybody. I hadn't even thought about what had happened or how it had happened. There's just this massive sense of loss and we all just need to wrap our arms around each other.

'This sounds a bit selfish but I was even thinking people are going to sit down and ask, "Suzy, are you okay? What happened to you on Friday …" It wasn't even brought up. Nothing was mentioned. I remember counsellors were arriving and I was thinking, "I would love to speak to somebody." But I was allowed maybe a maximum of five minutes. She asked me if I had an iPod, and told me I should listen to relaxing music and run a bath. And go on back to class.'

~

Suzy wasn't sure she was comfortable revisiting the death of Ainsley de Jong for this book. The toll that the accident took, and its after-effects, were real. But overriding any anxiousness and pain is a steadfast belief that doing what is right is what matters most.

Nearly a decade on, she understands how the de Jong family felt hurt, shunned and isolated by their school in the weeks and months after Ainsley's death. It was the school's reaction and handling of the situation that really eats away at Amanda de Jong, who says it made things so much harder at the time, and in the years ahead. Suzy understands what Amanda means.

'I definitely feel that,' Suzy says. 'I walked away from Willans Hill at that point. I was trying to deal with my own things of what went on that day … I was a single mum with five little people … and nothing felt right after that.'

She said in the immediate aftermath, she couldn't feel comfortable about conducting playground duty where Ainsley fell.

'I remember going back and thinking, "I don't want to be on that type of duty." I thought I would have leaders who would totally understand, but I felt I was looked at, like, "Why not?" It felt as though they were saying, "What a stupid thing to say to us." I felt I was brave to say that: "I'm not comfortable at the moment … maybe I will be okay but at the moment, I don't think I'm okay."

'In the end, I can't even remember exactly how my time ended, but I knew it wasn't a place I wanted to be at anymore. Which is a shame because I loved my work up there. I loved the students. I felt it was a fabulous little school that was enriching so many little people's lives. But after it all, nothing felt right and when there was an opportunity at another school, I took it and moved on, as bad as that sounds.'

Suzy moved schools, but she didn't leave it all behind.

'I had little kids at home. I used to look at my Archer [born just before Ainsley and her twin brother, Archie] and think, 'You're the same age as Ainsley. This is so unfair." I would have that feeling of, "How?" Through no fault of their own, they're burying their little girl, who was at a place where you hope they're safe. You send your kids to school and you never think they might not come home. That's the safe spot. I would think, if something like that, God forbid, ever happened to my child at school, I would like to think that the staff are supported better. It was like they were following the book on what to do, but where was the human element?'

The machine of bureaucracy had powered into gear – as evidenced by the timelines and information documenting exactly who was informed when and what actions were being taken – yet those on the ground, and at ground zero, in fact, seemed to be caught up in the wrong processes.

'It's the department of education. It's not a small business. There's hierarchy on hierarchy, people sitting in offices … one of them should've stepped in,' Suzy says, as she wrestles with the question of how it was that staff seemed to have been drafted into the wrong camp, where the focus was on looking after the organisation, rather than caring for the human beings.

'I remember thinking, 'Why aren't we just shutting the school, or putting movies on, and allowing teachers to cry or talk or just debrief … I felt I had so much I wanted to get off my chest and I didn't know how to get the words out – or get the opportunity. I just felt, as a person who worked at the school, as soon as we walked in on that Monday morning, it was game on. "There's a policy, there's a way we react. This is all you're allowed to do."'

She recalls the instruction to avoid contact with the family was explicit, with the explanation being that police and departmental investigations would have to take place.

'I can't remember exactly what was said, but I think I was asked why I had already been there. I said, "I know them. I'm not going to not go and see them. These people have lost a child. Why aren't we all there, or why aren't we all working out what we can do for them?" I didn't mean stuff that might be the responsibility of the department to work out, but just being good people and doing whatever you can. There's nothing you can do to bring back their daughter, but you can show them that we're here … that this is a nightmare and we want to help you through the nightmare. I think a lot of staff felt like, "Wow." But classes were back on Monday. I wasn't even the classroom teacher for Ainsley, and they were back in class on Monday morning and I remember thinking, "How?"

'I didn't care about the investigation going on. I was probably naive but I thought [our responsibility was] just to help people, be nice, and help make it as okay as it can be. It's a special school, too. There're kids in the class whose little friend wasn't going to turn up ever again. Shouldn't we be stopping and pausing for a moment? Holding some type of assembly? Acknowledging it … I felt like something should've been acknowledged. To me, it felt like, this bad thing happened, that was only on Friday. Now we're in a new week and, you know, we just go on. I remember thinking, "I can't." I can't get that picture out of my mind, and that sound. The noise at the hospital and what I saw.'

If Suzy hears of the death of a child now, particularly a death at school, her heart goes out not only to the family, but to all those around them … teachers and staff, classmates and fellow students, the broader school community, and paramedics attending the fatality of a young person.

'Not little kids. It hits differently with little kids. You're not meant to bury small people. It's not right,' she says. 'And Ainsley had had such a damn battle. For her to go that way, it just seemed so unfair – that she overcame so many obstacles and always came out the other end, then just to be taken in the playground on a bloody Friday afternoon …'

Ainsley was bigger than all that she endured, more than cancer victim or a schoolyard incident. Of that, Suzy is sure. That makes it hurt, too – that such a bright, bold, memorable personality could be reduced to the story of her own tragedy. Ainsley didn't deserve to be defined by her tumour, or the accident that took her life. It was her big heart and warm nature that should have been remembered: those defining characteristics of her strong and defiant spirit.

'I'm sure Aaron and Amanda play it in their heads over and over, pointlessly, thinking of scenarios like, "What if she'd stayed home that day?", "What if we picked her up at lunch?" I think to myself, "What if I was on duty at the time?" I knew her, maybe I would've been talking to her at the time and she wouldn't have been in that spot. All these silly little thoughts … "What if, what if, what if …" I just felt it was such a tragedy. Such a tragic event. Could it have been avoided? I don't know. I suppose everything could've been, to a degree, when you have hindsight. Hindsight's a wonderful thing.

'It's funny, but that Friday still sticks with me. We'll have mandatory CPR training and I'll be sitting there and in my head I'm thinking, "Nup, it's not like that. That's not how it works." That will stay with me forever. And it should.'

Sleepless nights and flashbacks were a part of life for Suzy for some time.

'I had them for a long time, until I went and got my own help. I just wasn't functioning well. I also felt guilty because I've got kids. All my kids are fine, they've been healthy,' she says. 'It sounds silly. I'm sure Aaron and Amanda would never think of me differently. But there was that guilt: how does one family the same age as me bury two children? It's so not fair. So not fair.'

~

The unfairness of it all – The Great Unfairness of It All – is like a tree. A living, growing organism reaching up and out, stretching limbs and branches skyward, spreading its shadow with time and within time – a shadow broadening by the year but waxing and waning with the travels of the sun and the passing of the seasons.

The tree of unfairness has its roots in Ainsley's personality, a wondrous place full of laughter and meaning. Such joy in a young child who spent her life disarming people with lightness and song is fertile ground.

But Ainsley herself was as a tree. A sacred tree, who encouraged wonder and awe; gatherings of warmth – of family, friends, supporters and strangers – as people admired her strength, her growth, and all that she offered to those in her vicinity. She was a delight – to teach, to know, to talk to and listen to; to love and to laugh with; to watch grow and learn; and to offer so much to all those around her.

Ainsley wasn't a person with a disability, or a tragedy that unfolded. She was life personified, where the meaning of life is in the giving, the sharing, the raising of spirits and lifting of others. She rose above pity, she changed the paradigm. And she was unforgettable.

Even in the end, despite the great unfairness of it all, that's what mattered more than anything else.

Reflection from Aaron

On the day of Ains' funeral, at the cemetery, a school staff member brought the parents of the kid that pushed Ains over and introduced them to Amanda. What the fuck?

Amanda being Amanda displayed her usual kindness and class and she didn't tell me till the next day. You can imagine why.

A few months later, Amanda was working at Coles and the same child's mother started going into the store and would just stare at Amanda working.

I'm not sure if she's not well or just a fucking moron but she did this several times. We got our solicitor to send a letter asking her to leave Amanda alone. The reply was a letter from her solicitor saying that it was a public place and she can shop wherever she likes. If that was me, I'd be avoiding it at all costs!

The day after this, she went in again. She was staring at Amanda and started laughing. Amanda, quite distressed by the situation, this time spoke up: 'Are you serious? Just fuck off.'

Understandably, she came home upset. I looked up their address from the police file I had and I drove around to the house. I was fired up and ready to punch her head in.

I bashed on the door so hard I think I wrecked it. A bloke came out looking very scared and I knew it wasn't her husband. He told me that they had moved. I apologised and left. It was probably a good thing because I was filthy and it wasn't going to end well.

Aaron de Jong, Ainsley's dad

CHAPTER 16

A very lonely experience

TRAUMA CREATES ITS own whirlpool of turmoil. The de Jongs found themselves living in a world few can understand. Not for the first time, Aaron says, nobody knew what to say.

'It's a very lonely experience. Even years after, people say the dumbest things. They don't mean it. They don't know,' he says. 'It's just a very lonely thing to go through.'

Aaron pinned his hopes for clarity on the coroner. The police paperwork was eventually completed but the trail quickly went cold.

'The Coroners Court basically said, "We've read the police report and we're happy with the findings. We can't see any reason to go to an inquest,"' Aaron says. 'I pestered them for years.'

In time, years of frustration, sadness and pain eventually boiled down to one burning question: how does a child go to school one Friday morning and finish the day in the hospital morgue? The pages and pages of information from the department of education included a line reporting that there'd been positive contact from the de Jong family towards the school in the week after Ainsley's death. But Aaron says the school was never forthcoming with information.

'We didn't hear anything from the school [about the day],' Aaron says. 'We didn't really know what had happened. It was only something I heard from what the police said they'd heard.'

~

The month after Ainsley Margaret de Jong died on school grounds in Wagga Wagga, the NSW cricketer Phillip Joel Hughes was killed during a game at the Sydney Cricket Ground in November 2014. In October 2016, the State Coroners Court of NSW held an inquest. Three weeks later, the findings were handed down.

Hughes' cause of death was traumatic basal sub-arachnoid haemorrhage. As for 'manner of death', the inquest found 'Phillip Hughes died from injuries sustained two days before his death when he was accidentally struck on the head by a ball bowled to him while he was batting in a first-class cricket match at the Sydney Cricket Ground.'

In Wagga Wagga, almost two years to the day since his daughter died, Aaron was at home, struggling with the seemingly inexplicable nature of her death. He was still hoping someone would search for the definitive truth about Ainsley's final hours. Unfolding in front of him was exactly what he knew *could* happen.

'You didn't have to ask people what happened [to Phillip Hughes] – you watched it. The whole country watched it. They flew people in from overseas and shut down the courts. The entire nation had the opportunity to see and hear exactly what happened,' he says. 'One of the hardest things for me is to read the paper and notice inquest after inquest being opened, giving families an opportunity to understand the circumstances of someone's death. I'm fine with that. What I'm not fine with is that there are some circumstances around Ains' death that need to be made available.'

Years later, Aaron remains mystified that the death of a child at school wasn't more closely examined. He made countless phone calls and sent regular emails to the Coroners Court.

'It seems other things get the attention that these types of incidents deserve, yet when it comes to my little girl, nobody seems to care,' he says. 'Having been told that there'd be an inquest a few months after the incident, I was surprised that I hadn't heard anything. I started chasing it up. When we spoke to our solicitor, John Potter, he laughed and told us that there wouldn't be an inquest, mainly because "We live in the country and it costs too much."'

~

On 5 July 2016, 'Mr & Mrs Aaron De Jong' were sent a letter from the Coroners Court of New South Wales. Headed 'Death of your daughter, Ainsley De Jong', the letter advised that the investigation into the circumstances of Ainsley's death was complete. The three pages were written and signed by Ann Lambino, Registrar, NSW State Coroners Court, on behalf of Deputy State Coroner Derek Lee. It declared: 'the Coroner thinks that it is not necessary to hold an inquest.'

The coroner had reviewed the police brief of evidence, including statements and documents gathered during their investigation, records obtained from Willans Hill School, and the post-mortem report. Given the role of the coroner is to make enquiries into sudden and unexpected deaths, five key questions need to be answered in the process: Who died? When did they die? Where did the death occur? What was the direct cause of death? And, what was the manner of the person's death? If those questions are answered, it says, there is usually no need for an inquest.

The letter points out that the Coroners Court doesn't resolve disputes between opposing parties, nor does it have the 'power to hold people or organizations [sic] to account. Civil courts, complaints authorities, ombudsmen and disciplinary tribunals do that work.'

The coroner identified four issues relating to student safety at Willans Hills School (WHS) but was satisfied with the knowledge of how Ainsley's death came about through witness statements and the autopsy report, and, medically, what caused her death. It also took into account 'improved safety measures that WHS has implemented' and intend to implement.

Willans Hill School had been invited to respond to four issues identified by the coroner relating to student safety:

1. *Whether an alternative playground surface, such as rubber softfall, might improve student safety*
   According to the coroner, 'WHS have advised that such an alternative surface has been considered but concerns have been raised about its suitability. The concerns relate to the fact that using a soft fall surface may make it difficult to move students who are in wheelchairs within the area …' The school advised it was exploring other options to reduce falls risks to students but the area of Ainsley's fall remained a concreted pebbled surface.
2. *Whether appropriate staff supervision of children in both the Junior and Senior playgrounds was in place*

The coroner noted that on 22 October 2014, five days after Ainsley's death, the school had updated the Student Behaviour Support Plan for one of the students involved in the incident, restricting him from the Junior playground. The investigation found that there were two supervising teachers for fewer than ten students in the Junior playground, that one was in Ainsley's immediate vicinity, and that the incident occurred without warning. The coroner said there were three adults supervising around 20 students in the Senior playground; however, because of students being spread out among the different areas of the playground, 'it was not logistically possible for the supervising teachers to maintain visual contact with all students at all times'.

3. *Whether it was possible to implement measures to keep students in the Junior playground area separated from older children in the Senior playground*
   On this matter, a logistical difficulty was noted, with the school toilets and library located within the junior playground area. Willans Hill School said it had taken steps to replace locks on the gates separating the playgrounds, to reduce the risk of unsupervised children moving between the playgrounds. (Specifically, the school's response 20 months after Ainsley's death was that it was 'currently obtaining quotes' and 'consultation with various suppliers' was taking place.)

4. *Whether it was possible to improve communication between school staff supervising children in the playground areas, particularly in the case of an emergency*
   Willans Hill School responded that the school is working with individual alarm suppliers to obtain quotes and advice on the use of alarms by teachers in the playgrounds.

~

Aaron was astounded by what he perceived as a shallow look into the four matters relating to student safety. He was livid about what he felt was a shallow investigation that merely scratched the surface of the issues and accepted responses without question.

The letter from the Coroners Court went on to explain the decision not to hold an inquest:

> The main reason for holding an inquest is to find out what caused an unexpected death. In Ainsley's case we know, from the witness statements that have been collected by the police and the autopsy report, how it came about. We also know the medical cause of her death. Having considered all of the available evidence, and taking into account the improved safety measures that WHS has implemented (and intend to implement), the Coroner has not been able to identify

> any issue that would require an inquest to be held. For these reasons, the coroner [sic] thinks that it is not necessary to hold an inquest.

~

In the autopsy report prepared for the coroner, there is no escaping Ainsley's brain tumour. It's referenced on three of the five pages of a heart-wrenching document, date-stamped as being received in Wagga on '12 Dec 2014'.

On the cover page, which outlines who Ainsley was, and details the who, when and where of the autopsy, the seven-year-old girl is spared the burden of her illness. She's simply 'Ainsley Margaret De Jong, a female born 07.12.06, identified by her wristband to the pathologist, Dr Allan David CALA'. But Ainsley's tumour is everywhere else, including reference in the 'disease or condition leading to death': 'Blunt force head injury in a child with pilocytic astrocytoma.'

It's also mentioned as background in the first few paragraphs of the autopsy report's 'Circumstances of Death', which notes the information provided at the time of autopsy was taken from the police form P79a – Report of Death to the Coroner:

> This 7 year old girl had been diagnosed with a pilocytic astrocytoma (a malignant brain tumour especially

> affecting children) at age 4 months. The tumour was known to have been based around the pituitary fossa at the base of the brain and was known to have spread throughout the nervous system with spinal metastases present.
>
> She had undergone surgery followed by chemotherapy and radiation therapy at Sydney Children's Hospital, Randwick, and was under the care of an oncologist in Sydney. She last underwent chemotherapy treatment two weeks prior to her death. She had severe visual impairment and moderate intellectual disability.
>
> At the time of her death, she was attending Willans Hill School in Wagga Wagga. This is [a] school which caters for children with intellectual and other disabilities. She had been residing with her parents and siblings in the family home at Wagga.

It *is* background. Because the tumour didn't actively take Ainsley's life. The report continues:

> During the lunch break on 17.10.14, Ainsley was in the playground and had been picking flowers. Another child pushed her to the upper chest region, causing her to fall backwards. The back of Ainsley's head struck a concrete surface. A teacher who had been present immediately went to her aid but by then, Ainsley was not moving.

The autopsy report records that Ainsley was unconscious and 'gulping' for air by the time other staff arrived at her side, and that her condition deteriorated. By the time an ambulance and her father, Aaron, arrived on the scene, she was without a pulse, and:

> CPR was commenced and she was conveyed to Wagga Base Hospital. She was immediately attended to by doctors and intubated. She had a cardiac arrest and was unable to be revived, with life pronounced extinct at 3.50pm.

An external examination in the presence of police and a brain CT scan were performed. An irregularly shaped area of abrasion was noted at the back of Ainsley's scalp, under which was scalp bruising. The CT scan at hospital showed the large pre-existent tumour, with shunt. It also showed acute subdural bleeding.

For all the impact of that pilocytic astrocytoma on Ainsley's life, and the ever-present nature of its existence – right through to the autopsy report into her death – it was a shove, a fall, abrasions, bruising and bleeding that ultimately told her final story.

The report says:

> It seems likely the child sustained severe head impact trauma when she landed on a hard concreted surface.

> This appears to have caused a sudden but severe 'jolt' to the brain resulting in almost immediate loss of consciousness and cardiac arrest soon after.

The report notes three items under evidence of injury: a collection of fine linear abrasions of 50 millimetres in diameter at the back of Ainsley's head; three faint purple-red bruises on her right upper forehead in an area 25 × 15 millimetres; and a yellowed abrasion 40 millimetres in diameter on her left shoulder.

The autopsy report offered plenty of medical detail and some explanation about the cause of Ainsley's death. But Aaron was adamant the coroner hadn't given a full explanation as to what went wrong, and how, in the schoolyard playground two Octobers earlier. The initial letter sent on behalf of Deputy State Coroner Derek Lee invited the de Jongs to submit in writing to the Coroners Court any concerns they held which they believed could only be addressed in an inquest.

Two weeks later – some 21 months after Ainsley died – the de Jongs did just that, via a letter from their solicitor, John Potter. In particular, they queried whether the available evidence could allow for a finding to be made about the manner of Ainsley's death, and questioned the lack of clarification about a possible second fall or incident involving Ainsley after she was initially shoved to the ground. There were big questions, too, in Aaron's mind as to how and why an older male student was able to be in a playground where he apparently sparked the chain of events on 17 October 2014

On 12 August 2016, Ann Lambino, registrar at the NSW State Coroners Court, responded on behalf of Deputy State Coroner Derek Lee. The coroner was adamant the manner of Ainsley's death was explained: 'That is, it occurred from a fall after she was pushed by another student.'

He accepted there was evidence in the statement from the teacher nearest to Ainsley in the playground, Janelle Urbanivicius, that it was apparent that Ainsley had moved after her initial fall. However, the coroner insisted that didn't necessarily mean there was a 'second fall', merely referencing 'an assumption … that there actually was a second fall due to the change in Ainsley's position.'

He noted the witness did not know how the change in position came about, evidence she was clear about in her statement and in a later walk-through video with police. The coroner believed 'any evidence at inquest will not further our understanding of how Ainsley came to be in a different position after her fall'.

The de Jongs and John Potter also queried the action taken by the school since the accident, believing the coroner had simply accepted the school's responses to its four key issues, even though very little change had been implemented after Ainsley's death.

Nearly two years on, the coroner acknowledged some measures being considered by Willans Hill School hadn't yet been implemented, but said action was taken to identify and address the issues and it was ongoing. The coroner then reiterated that at no point would he ever have the power to compel the school to make changes:

> Even if an inquest was held, the Coroner only has the power to make recommendations. The Coroner has no power to compel Willans Hill to actually implement any of the measures that they are considering, or to do so by a certain date. For this reason, the Coroner does not think that an inquest, or any recommendation, would advance the action that is currently underway.'

As to Ainsley's fall itself, and her pre-existing medical conditions, the coroner said he had sought further advice from the forensic pathologist who conducted Ainsley's autopsy, Dr Cala, and from Dr John Lawson, a paediatric neurologist recommended by Ainsley's oncologist. Both advised it was not possible to say whether a softer playground surface would have made Ainsley's death preventable. Dr Lawson's opinion was that the force of the push was a more important factor to consider.

The coroner believed an inquest would be unable to take that matter any further either. Furthermore, the response from the court dismissed the idea raised by Mr Potter that issues in Ainsley's case held general importance throughout the school system, particularly for children with special needs and vulnerabilities, declaring:

> However, the Coroner has not been able to identify evidence that Ainsley's death was the result of a systemic failing within the school system. The Coroner is of the opinion that there is insufficient evidence for an inquest to consider such a broad issue.
>
> For the above reasons, the Coroner remains of the view that an inquest is not required and he intends to dispense with holding an inquest.

~

The inquest into the death of cricketer Phillip Hughes later that year, in October 2016, illustrated what an alternative path might have looked like for the de Jongs. In the introduction to his findings released in December 2016, State Coroner Michael Barnes noted that 'a coroner may make such recommendations considered necessary or desirable in relation to any matter connected with the death, including in relation to public health and safety'. He said there was no doubt about the date and time of Hughes' death and 'the focus of this inquest has been upon the manner and cause of death, and whether any recommendations should be made'.

The inquest was to cover everything from the rules of the game and the nature of play to the safety equipment used by players, and the emergency planning and response to Hughes' injury. His findings noted that an inquest was 'not a forum for determining civil liability, or for apportioning blame. It is an opportunity to expose the facts of the matter, with a focus on considering any steps that might be taken to prevent similar deaths occurring, or to protect cricketers from such risks, in the future.'

The coroner added that the 'investigation is focused on providing a greater understanding of what happened on the day Phillip was fatally injured and identifying reforms and improvements to the protection of cricketers and in emergency responses'.

~

In the autumn of the next year, in March and April 2017, Aaron de Jong was still emailing the state coroner begging for an inquest to be opened into his daughter's death at the special needs school. Aaron said he held real concerns for the safety of other children at the school and expressed his 'anger and frustration that after two and a half years I really have no answers'. He said there had still been no explanation as to how an older student – whose management plan explicitly stated he was not allowed in

Ainsley, with her trademark twinkle in the eyes and smile on her face, in between bouts of chemotherapy.

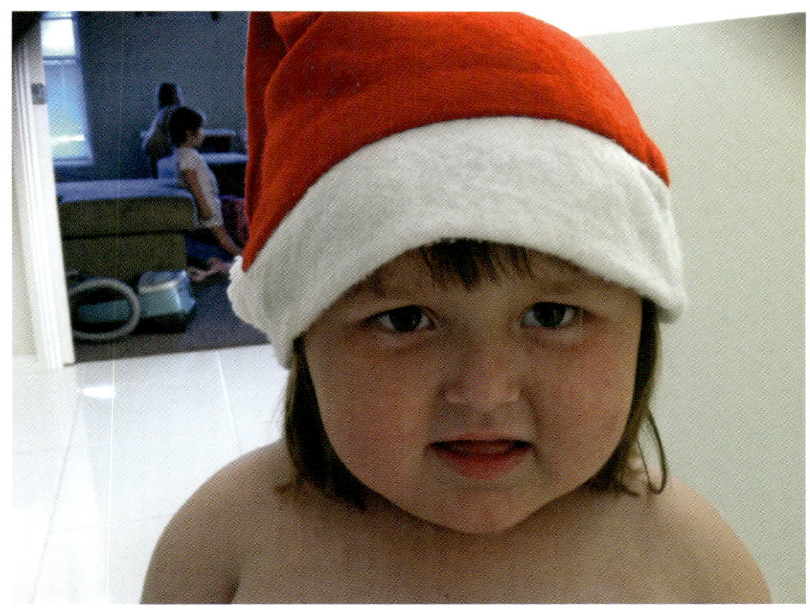

Merry Christmas!

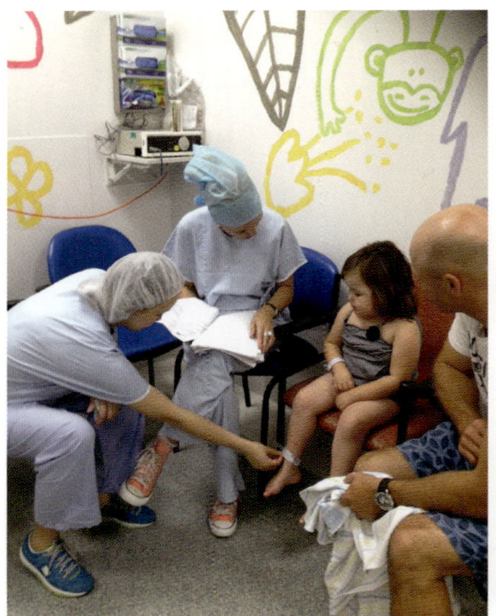

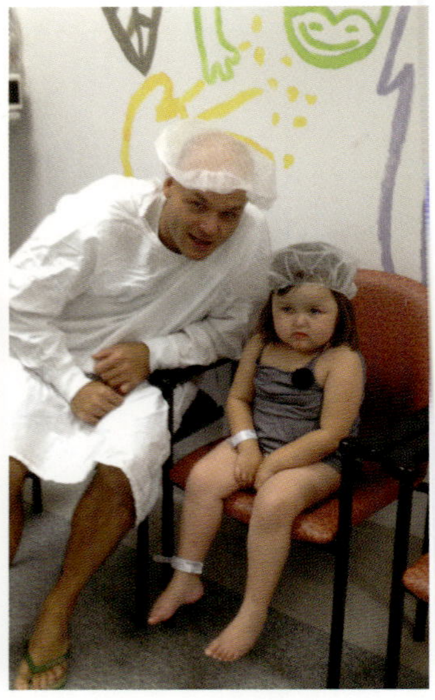

Ainsley with dad Aaron by her side as she and the medical staff prepare for another operation to relieve pressure in her brain.

Back at school, however, there was no stopping Ains. With Dolly in support, she performs the Wishy Washy Washer Woman at the end of year concert in 2013.

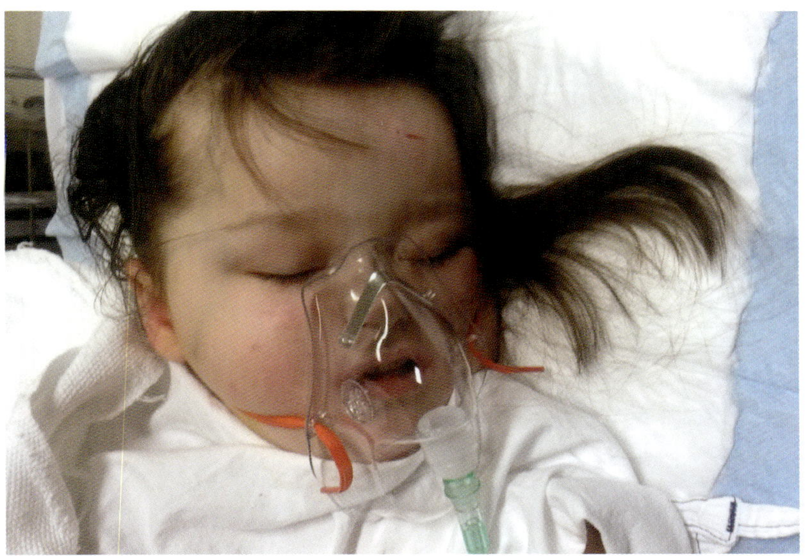

Whether it was treatments of chemotherapy or operations to relieve the pressure caused by her brain tumour, Ainsley was more than familiar with the routines of medical treatment...

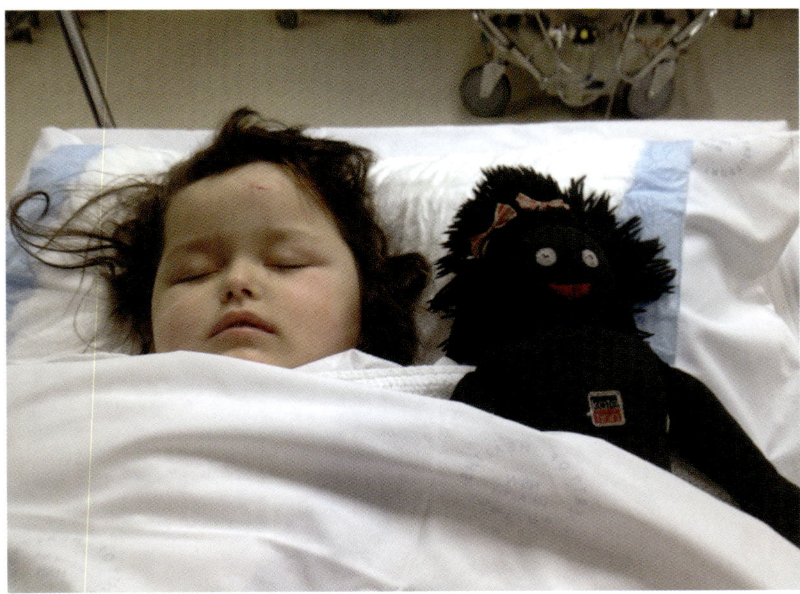

... and with her trusty sidekick Dolly, she bounced back time and again, living up to the confidence her parents placed in her, that she would defy grim outlooks and expectations.

Ains, Addi and Aud hanging out together in hospital.

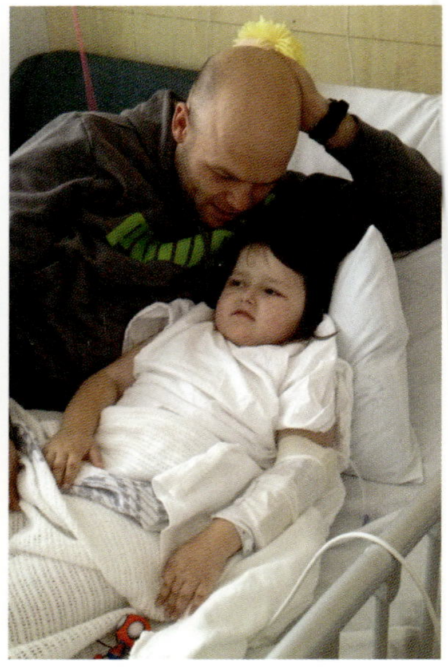

Aaron and Ainsley.

Amanda and Ains share a moment of joy in a hospital waiting room.

Addi and Aud doing their best to lift Ains' spirits during a photo shoot on a day when Ainsley's illness had knocked her flat.
(Photograph: Skye Rocket Studio)

No-one could laugh like Ainsley de Jong, and a day out at the Batemans Bay Show in 2014 saw her in full flight.

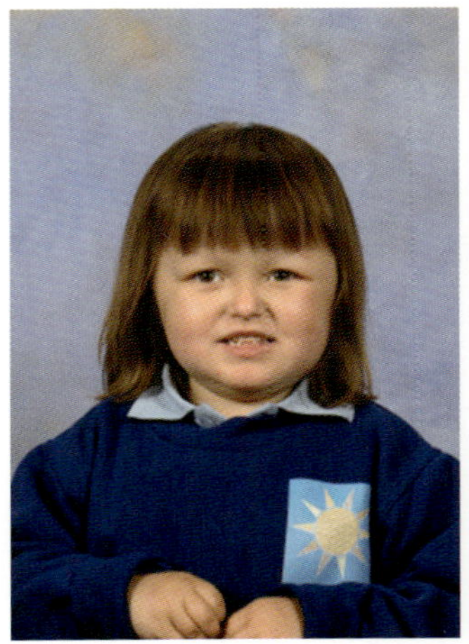

School photo time.
Ainsley was thriving in her learning and development at Willans Hill School.

She thrived on school dress-up days too!

Ains with Aud, Addi and Amanda on their holiday to the NSW South Coast in 2014.

Aaron with his three daughters on their final family holiday.

Ains surrounded by her parents and sisters in their last family photo together.

Ains takes Dolly on a day out to picturesque Lilli Pilli Beach in Batemans Bay.

Dolly was Ainsley's support through the tough times, her sidekick in fun and her friend in need. Dolly and Ains lie together, forever.

the junior playground – came to be in the area where he sparked a confrontation that started the chain of events that led to Ainsley being pushed over.

Aaron said there needed to be an increase in the number of staff supervising the playgrounds, given Deputy State Coroner Derek Lee's observation that 'it was not logistically possible for the supervising teachers to maintain visual contact with all students at all times'. Aaron felt the Coroners Court had too freely accepted the school's responses that, some two years after the incident, it was 'working with suppliers to obtain quotes and advice about the use of alarm systems'; that it had dismissed 'using soft fall as a playground surface on the basis that it would be difficult for moving wheelchairs', and merely mentioned it was 'exploring other options to reduce falls risks'.

It was unfathomable to Ainsley's parents that a child had died and two years later, next to nothing had happened in response. So long had passed, in fact, that by now Aaron had his copy of files released by the Department of Education. He could see the department's response to the original WorkCover investigation two-and–a-half years earlier, and he could read the answer to the final question himself:

> 13. Has any procedure or system of work been reviewed/modified as a result of the incident?

> 'Systems of playground monitoring and behaviour risk management have been reviewed but no modification has been identified as necessary.'

Is it any wonder that Aaron's emotional state and mental health were spiralling?

PART 4

I have always felt that a human being could only be saved by another human being.

I am aware that we do not save each other very often.

But I am also aware that we save each other some of the time.

James Baldwin, *Nothing Personal*, 1964

CHAPTER 17

It broke the both of them, too

On the south-eastern edge of the city's suburbs, the Wagga Wagga Lawn Cemetery is an immaculately kept oasis of green. It's peaceful, quiet and calm. In the right weather, at the right time of year, you can turn your back on the sunset to see a full moon rising over section 7, where Ainsley and Archie de Jong are at rest.

On the left of a shared headstone is a drawing of a little boy with a pair of angel's wings and the inscription 'SO SMALL, SO SWEET, SO SOON' to remember Archie. On the other side is a photo of a smiling Ainsley in her element – all spunk, cheek and joy – with the words above, 'KEEP ON DANCING BABY GIRL'.

Aaron visits often, to sit at the side-by-side graves of his lost twins.

'I visit Ains and Archie every week. I tell them what we've been up to each week. I missed a few weeks when we were on holidays. I also fell asleep half-pissed on the grass one day in the sunshine,' he says.

He and Amanda have been to hell and back since Ainsley died. Aaron's perception of a lack of interest from the Coroners Court drove him to desperation, and almost to the unthinkable.

'Twice when I was wide awake and doing countless miles in my head, I drove to the street next to the school,' he says. 'I was wound up, frustrated, and had thoughts of driving my car straight through the front gates of the school in the hope that it might get some publicity and force the issue. Put simply, the coroners are fucking arseholes! The way they operate is an absolute joke.'

Processing the trauma in the intervening years, Aaron has thought deeply about the impact of losing their daughter, re-examining not just her life and the circumstances of her death, but the circle of sorrow, too. Like ripples from a stone thrown into still water, the trauma comes in waves of concentric circles … one small tide followed by another, then another, then another.

'My parents are "old school",' he says. 'This is probably a by-product of their upbringing. Dad's family fled Holland during the Second World War with nothing. My nan, who was in a wheelchair with polio, raised my mum with very little support. Mum's dad disappeared when she was young and she's never seen him since. Both Mum and Dad don't often talk about what happened with Ains and, whenever they do, they often cry. It's hard for them and for me to know what to say. Ains dying broke the both of them, too. It has been hard for me to watch. In saying that, they're the first to be there for us, they'll help with anything and I'll never be able to thank them enough.'

The same, and more, can be said for his wife. Aaron realised that even a tight-knit couple will have their own individual response to facing their inner turmoil, and finding their own path past the obstacles put in their way.

'Over the years, I've learned that everyone deals with their stuff differently – this isn't necessarily a bad thing. For Amanda, she rarely cries and attempts to create the impression that she's going okay,' he says. 'The reality of it all is that she lives two lives. Everyone thinks she is flying but that's definitely not the case. But she is strong, probably too strong for her own good.'

Strong enough to sustain the two of them?

'To be perfectly honest, and I don't say it lightly, if it wasn't for Amanda, I wouldn't be here.'

Aaron counts himself lucky on a few fronts. As well as his wife, his family and close friends, there's his successful business, Nugent and Andrea Jewellers in Wagga Wagga's main street. Nowadays, he has mixed emotions about his work, but beyond the business there's the friendship and support of an understanding partner, Paul Andrea.

If it takes a village to raise a child, as the saying goes, it takes a community to throw its arms around a suffering adult.

'Over the journey, Paul, my business partner, has been really supportive of my situation,' he says. 'I talk with him about some things and, while it doesn't get too heavy, I know we will be mates forever. Paul and I have a great business that we worked bloody hard to establish but I hate myself every day I go into the shop. When Ains was crook or had an appointment, I was always thinking about getting back to work. It still gets me down a lot. About 18 months after Ains died, I had a breakdown, basically started an argument and took off.

'Paul was really understanding but also knew I had to get help. He rang Amanda, to tell her I wasn't in a good way. Amanda was working at the time so she rang Mum and Dad and they came to check in on me. I wish they had never seen me in the state I was in as I could see how upset it made them.'

Aaron has considered stepping away from the business plenty of times. But he also wants to be a loyal business partner and friend in return. Amanda says, taking everything into account in those years after Ainsley's death, it was tempting at times to let go of the questioning, the wondering and the search of answers. She almost begged her husband to.

'Part of me was like, "Just give it up, Aaron. We've got to try and get past this." But he wasn't giving up. It was hard. I knew why he was doing it but … fuck!'

Amanda's exasperation wasn't entirely for Aaron. Somewhere within, when she was honest with herself, she knew she was only just hanging on. She was keeping her guard up and her emotions buried, sometimes for the wrong reasons.

'I used to wonder what people might think or say,' she says. 'I was worried about the girls and protecting the family, I guess.'

Amanda never did insist to Aaron that they try to move on and leave it all behind, tempting as that thought was at times. Underneath her get-on-with-business attitude – motivated by a need to stay on top of things so she could care for Addison and Audrey – Amanda also had a more-than-nagging feeling that Ainsley's death hadn't been dealt with adequately or fairly.

'I knew that's how I felt. But I was so drained with all of it,' Amanda says. 'But it all started when the coroner wasn't going to do an inquest. It all just started … that's when the anger really kicked in. I got to a point where I felt something has to be done. Nobody would put their hand up and say, "We stuffed up." I think if the school had gone about it better, or sat us down and talked about it, or admitted something went wrong … it might have been different. In the end, we wanted to go to court, because we wanted to get Ainsley's story out.'

Dissatisfied with the coroner's decision to dispense with holding an inquest, the de Jongs believed pursuing a civil case themselves was their only option if they wanted Ainsley's death, and its aftermath, to be comprehensively and publicly explored.

Time by M. Vasalis

I dreamed that I was living slowly,
More slowly than an ancient stone –
A nightmare: above me, around me, below me
All shook, twitched, sprouted. I alone
was still. I saw the urgent force
that split the soil as trees burst free,
singing in voices cracked and hoarse.
Each season flew off after the others:
a dizzying whirl of rainbow colors.
I saw the trembling of the sea,
its swelling and its hasty shrinking,
a giant gullet always drinking.
Day vanished into night and came
alight again like flickering flame.
Those gesturing things showed such intense
desperation and eloquence,
awoken from paralysis
to struggle, wild and merciless ...
How could it be I never guessed,
I never saw the truth till now?
I must forget again – but how?

First published in 1940
(English translation by David McKay, 2020)

CHAPTER 18

I'll feel I've let her down

AINSLEY'S FAMILY HAVE moved from her old house with her favourite flight of stairs to a place on a hill on the outskirts of Wagga Wagga. In wintertime, the house can sit above a sea of fog when it rolls in in the early hours of a brisk morning to blanket everything below, bar the odd light bravely flickering through the cloud of water droplets. It can offer a sense of calm, this clear view eastward to the rising sun while all below is hidden – the hustle and bustle of households, neighbourhoods, half a city preparing for the day in the half-light of fog. Inner turmoil silenced and a settled head above the clouds.

Inside the house on the hill, the de Jongs' eldest daughter has a room of her own, which her sisters and parents walk past daily. Ainsley's favourite pink Nike joggers are in the cupboard. A beautiful photo of her as a baby, all wrinkles and skin and a smiling face, adorns the wall. There are photos and tributes given by family and friends and a framed certificate of a star named after Ainsley, with a map showing the exact location of the celestial object, a little to the right of the star that sits at the base of the Southern Cross.

One of Ainsley's beloved jumpsuits has been sewn into a cushion cover on the bed, sitting alongside another pillow covered in one of her school t-shirts. There's no Dolly among the cushions and toys in the bed, or the personal items in the cupboards. Dolly lies with Ainsley.

~

It seemed extraordinary, but legal action felt like the only course of action left open for a couple determined to seek more information about what occurred on that searingly painful afternoon, to find out exactly what happened on 17 October 2014 – a Friday that had started out like any other ordinary school day.

Aaron remembers a typical spring day, a cool morning developing into a mild and sunny afternoon. He wore a vest over his t-shirt when he headed off to work.

Amanda, meanwhile, still shudders at the thought as a ripple of unease passes through her body and she recalls being terribly unwell. It's a visceral feeling, and a haunting memory that won't be forgotten.

'The day she died, the fact that I was in bed sick was weird. Just weird,' Amanda says. 'You look back and wonder, was that a sign? I was never sick. I didn't have time to be. But that day, I felt sick all day. Now, if I don't feel well, I can't go to bed.'

Amanda prefers to remember the joyous times. The image that invariably comes to mind when she thinks of Ainsley is her little girl up and dancing in the school concerts.

'That was the best. They're the days that I like to remember,' she says.

~

Legal action was its own little nightmare as years passed with little to show for it. In 2020, finally, there were some answers. What they discovered through launching their own action, as Aaron recounts, is that: 'A primary school boy had got into the junior playground and when the teacher told him that he wasn't supposed to be there, he then slapped another girl who had a history of being aggressive. The teacher on duty saw this and started to walk the girl to a classroom. As they walked past Ains, the girl pushed her hard with both hands in the chest, she fell back and smashed her head in the concrete. The teacher left Ains on the ground, continued to escort the other girl to the classroom, then went back to Ains who was unconscious. She then tried to wave and get the attention of an autistic child to go get help.'

Aaron finds the same question always comes begging in his mind when he thinks about it: 'I mean, for fuck's sake, everyone's got a mobile phone in their pocket, don't they?' He could never understand why the call for help wasn't made immediately.

While the court case helped uncover some details, it was far from a satisfactory experience.

'The whole civil case is another shit show that takes lots of time and money,' Aaron says. 'Ours took five years! Further to this was the fact that our cases were separate from each other's and, because Amanda gritted her teeth, got going with work and life, as Amanda does, they rated her loss half as substantial as mine. This was an enormous kick in the guts for her. This was her way of dealing with the grief of losing Ains. We both dealt with things differently and I know Amanda is hurting just as much as me.'

Exorbitant costs, the time involved and the use of expert witnesses on both sides to support arguments left the de Jongs with something of a sour taste of their experience.

'I suppose what we wanted most out of the case was for people to know the truth about Ainsley's death. Even now, most people still think she died of brain cancer,' Aaron says. 'Before going to court, the advice was to try and resolve our grievance through mediation. We built ourselves up for a positive result and they basically just offered us money … $200,000 to go away. We wanted to push on with a court case so we could get some actual answers. They then wanted another mediation. We went again and, not surprisingly, they offered a bit more money. We once again declined as, for us, it wasn't about the money.'

By then, it was early in 2020. COVID-19 had arrived. The de Jongs were told only eight people would be allowed in court, including the judges, barristers and lawyers. That meant no media, and that meant no exposure of their daughter's story.

A final offer came three days before the court date. Aaron refused it, only to be argued against strongly by his own legal team, warning him that he may not do their own case any favours by carrying his anger into a civil case. He was even tested, prodded by searching questions and leading statements from his lawyer. When he reacted, raging against the insinuations and suggestions, Aaron recognised the 'I told you so' reaction he received.

He was an uncoachable witness and, no matter how good his reasons for being honest, open and raw, and his determined desire to expose the flaws and failures in the systems they'd encountered, it wasn't going to help. Aaron tried to insist that in court, when he knew what was coming, he would be able to contain himself.

For Amanda, the warnings of what lay ahead were a serious concern.

'If what they were saying was going to happen,' she says, 'like get Aaron on the stand and absolutely rip into him [and] get me on the stand and tell me I was doing better now that my daughter had passed, things like that, I thought, "I can't go through that. I can't live through that." I said to Aaron, we've got to think of the girls. They're older. They're at school. We didn't know whether there was going to be media or not. I don't know. It all just got too much. Even the whole process, it felt like every door that opened would then close and it felt like we were never going to get what we wanted. Our story was never going to be told through court. That was what we'd thought and why we'd kept pushing, because we wanted the truth to come out.'

Ultimately, Aaron realised he would have to park his indignation, however much it hurt, and accept the legal advice, and accept the settlement.

'After that, with all of the COVID restrictions in place, after much thought and many tears, we felt that nobody was going to hear Ains' story anyway through the case. We settled with them the day before court,' he says. 'I remember the solicitor rang and said, "Aaron, your case is closed."' That was that. 'I still find it hard to fathom that, after all the carry-on that continued for more than five years, it was sorted within a few hours. It's almost like the barristers get a kick out of it,' Aaron says.

He and Amanda maintain that pursuing legal action was never about money. There was no value that could be placed on Ainsley's life and what was lost. It was about accountability and answers after being devastated at every turn and by every departmental process they encountered after Ainsley's death.

Aaron says the one thing they demanded in a settlement was the right to speak about it. After all they'd been through, they would never agree to being silenced.

'I do think we did the right thing in letting go as Ains' story wasn't going to be heard as publicly as we would have liked,' Aaron says. 'But still, I'd like to tell her story to the wider public. If I don't, I know I'll feel as though I've let her down.'

From Ainsley's Eulogy

Our journey with Ainsley is now over and we will miss her terribly.

Ainsley was a delight and is irreplaceable. It has been a true privilege to care for Ainsley and one we all will never forget.

Ainsley, it is time for Mum, Dad, Addi, Audrey, Omie, Op, Poppy, and all your adoring aunts, uncles and cousins to say goodbye.

We will cherish the memories and hold you close in our hearts forever.

To our beautiful darling little girl, we will never forget you and we will love you forever.

Carol Cattell, Paediatric Outreach Nurse, Wagga Wagga Base Hospital
Sacred Heart Church, October 2014

CHAPTER 19

A search for meaning

THERE WAS NO victory dance or feeling of vindication after the pre-court settlement. An emptiness remains, still.

There have been some explanations, and some satisfaction in knowing that, even by launching their own action, the Willans Hill School and NSW Department of Education had been forced to review their procedures and, internally perhaps, account for what happened on the school grounds.

The Department of Education records also showed the Coroners Court had at least returned to the matter and followed up the school's actions.

The de Jongs could see that in July 2016 there were records of phone calls, emails and meetings at the school, and a new principal implemented new administrative control measures to try to reduce the likelihood of another similar incident, including changes to playground areas, extra supervision and modified break times.

Buried deep in that trove of 133 pages of information, supplied under freedom of information obligations, was an orb of Ainsley's spirit, glowing with her love of sound and rhythm. The records of her medical history, supplied to Willans Hill School prior to her enrolment, included a 2010 assessment of Ainsley. It noted that at three years and four months of age, she was developmentally delayed, significantly in some areas, due to her tumour. But Ainsley 'was often observed to dance, although there was no music playing', 'singing to her encouraged her attention and co-operation' and 'Ainsley particularly enjoys music which can be used to settle her'.

Ainsley's rapid improvement was also evident, with a subsequent medical report in early 2011 noting a small decrease in her tumour, great improvement in her social skills and physical movement, and reporting that she 'looked very well' ahead of a sixth cycle of chemotherapy, a year before she started school.

~

The de Jongs' emotions remain thoroughly mixed when it comes to the school that took their little girl in. Aaron can still hear the words: 'She will be safe here.' But he knows what they gave her, too.

'Even after what happened to Ains,' he says, 'I still believe it was such a good place for her. Within a couple of years, she had learned to communicate, spell, know her numbers and do sign language. She also made some friends, too. I'm not sure if she knew they were her friends but she would mention them at home sometimes!'

Still, he felt himself unravelling in the weeks, months and years after Ainsley's death. At times it was like living a life outside himself. Not that swirling out-of-body experience that overtook him in the gravest moments, but an unsettling feeling that you no longer quite fit.

'One of the hardest things for me', he says, 'was seeing people soon after Ains died. I've seen people I know cross the street just to ensure they don't run into me. I don't blame them, they just don't know what to say and to be honest, most of the time, it's probably better off!

'Other times, I can sense people feeling sorry for me and that also feels bad. And of course, there're the times when someone starts talking about Ains and I spend the whole time saying, "Thank you" and "It's okay." Before long, they're the ones crying and I'm the one comforting them! I've also heard some people say they "should have been there for us", but to be honest, I'm not actually sure what that means. And it's hard to explain your own lived experience as a response when it's suggested, "You should have said something."

'Both of us had little time to process and grieve for Archie, as Ains got sick not long after she was born. And from there, the rollercoaster had already started.'

Amanda has handled the years without Ainsley in a different manner to her husband, but it doesn't mean they're in different places. She, too, remains perplexed that the death of their daughter – a schoolgirl, on school grounds – could pass with so little public comment or accountability.

'People still think she died of brain cancer. It's weird,' she says. 'That's what pissed me off more. "No! She was fighting that. She was a fighter. This is what happened." And people would say, "I didn't hear about that", or "I didn't know about that."'

To an extent, Amanda buried her heart and her anger in the early days, conscious that Addison and Audrey needed her as much as Ainsley had. And she needed them.

'I think my focus was Addi and Aud, to keep me going. I knew I had to. I think my grief with Ainsley didn't really start back then [when she died]. It was just another roller coaster, like with Archie, and I just didn't have the time. I had Aaron going through his stuff, I had the girls to worry about, someone had to go to work. He was having issues with his business. And with court on top of that.

'I think my worst days were through all the legal action. They were my days when I thought, "I can't do this anymore."' Generally, however, Amanda pushed it all back down, deep enough that she knew the complications of grief would be contained for now. But deep enough, too, that it sat next to a knot of truth; one that told her there would be a time and a place for reckoning to come. Until then, she would keep her head down and push on, for the girls' sake.

'I often thought it was a good thing that I didn't start grieving then. But I'm starting to think it was maybe not so good.'

Amanda, like Aaron, is relieved that the processes of Ainsley's death are behind them. There will never be closure. There won't be a 'moving on'. Why would there be? But there can be meaning, and that's what she'd like.

'I think it had to stop,' she says. 'I'm not sure how we could've coped otherwise. Aaron wasn't easy to live with for a little while. But I understood. In a way, I'm glad it ended the way it did. But at the same time, I'm with him. Something needs to be said, to be put out there. I think if it's in our words, not in court, that's better.'

~

The Canadian writer and historian Michael Ignatieff has turned his attention late in his career to the concept of consolation. Speaking about his 2021 book *On Consolation*, Ignatieff says men and women across time have looked to each other to recover hope and resilience but there is a difference between comfort and consolation. Consolation is about finding meaning, so that suffering can be borne. Ignatieff says whether it's what is said to us or what we tell ourselves, consolation must be honest. It can't be part of a 'ritual of politeness', or saying things we don't believe. It requires trust. And when a tragic circumstance defies explanation, what matters then is to be with good people.

~

In the intervening years, Aaron has plumbed the depths in an effort to work out where to start if he's to rebuild. A significant step was therapy, and a major regret is that it was two years after Ainsley died before he sought professional help. He is rebuilding himself, but knows it will be a lifelong project.

'In 2017, my sister in-law had a baby and commented that Amanda and I should go to the hospital and visit,' he says. 'As soon as this was mentioned, I felt a knot manifesting in my guts. As we arrived at the hospital, my heart started pumping hard and I was sweating like a pig. I legged it to the toilet and started vomiting. Amanda knocked on the door to make sure I was okay. I asked her to go and visit Franky and said that I'd meet her at home.

'I put my head under the tap to try and cool myself down and when I finally departed, I was all over the shop. The next thing I remember was two people assisting me up from a garden in the carpark of the hospital. They must have thought I was off my head on drugs and, when I realised they were trying to take me back inside, I palmed them off and got to my car. I drove around the corner, caught my breath and cried …

'It scared the absolute hell out of me. It probably comes as no surprise that this sort of occurrence can happen to someone diagnosed with post-traumatic stress disorder and anxiety. The first few years were really bad with the flashbacks. The best way I can describe them is similar to the moments in the Bourne movies, where Jason Bourne is trying to rediscover his past. These moments pop up in front of you and, for me personally, it's frightening.

'The flashbacks happen pretty randomly. Sometimes, they can happen quite frequently, while other times, I won't have had one for a while and something will trigger me off again. The other thing I deal with is nightmares. Amanda will wake me at night, after I've been screaming, yelling or just crying loudly. When I wake up, my heart is pumping and I'm sweating. On occasions, even my daughters have asked why I was yelling and swearing in the night. These days, I'm not as keen to take a weekend away with mates. Apart from the anxiety of being away from Amanda and the girls, these episodes could make a weekend away a bit awkward.

'Sleep is my biggest battle. I'm able to get to sleep, but not for long. And when I'm awake my mind is always racing. I'm often finding myself up and showering at 2 am and the flow-on effect is that I've always got a headache and I'm always tired! I've tried yoga and every sleeping pill I can find and after a while, it starts to wear me down to the point where I just take enough pills to knock me out. Not surprisingly, this results in a hangover that I pay for the next day. For me, however, it does at the very least feel like my mind has had a break.

'Similar to Amanda, I've found it's easier bouncing between two lives. When I'm away from home, I try to be as normal as I can and engage with others when I have to. I'm conscious of trying not to mope. It isn't easy. But when I get home, I'm able to relax and enjoy the time I spend with Amanda and the girls. Even more so since buying a little hobby farm at the end of 2018. The farm is another thing that has saved me. I've been able to spend a lot more time on my own which, for me, comes easy.

'I enjoy my own time and have the added benefit of the girls being nearby. But it's also easier to avoid the public situations that agitate and anger me. Petty things, people doing anything to look important. Or things like seeing a mother and daughter crying after losing an Under 11 game of netball, or listening to people in coffee shops whingeing about the quality of their coffee like it's the worst thing that's happened to them. It takes all my energy to walk out instead of saying something… or just burying their face into the counter!

'Put simply, I am nothing like the person I used to be. Not just for the above reasons but for many others. Life is very much consumed with thoughts of Ains and Archie and something as straightforward as somebody suggesting a "family photo" gives me a pain in the stomach. It hurts so much because, once again, it feels like people have forgotten that all of my family isn't physically there. For me, there'll never be another complete family photo and that's hard to accept.

'These days, I'm content doing the same stuff every day. I eat the same foods. At the same time, I don't have any grand goals and I'm just happy to be an "average Joe". As long as Amanda and the kids are happy, to me, nothing else matters. I used to be very confident, driven, outgoing, selfish, really, and I wanted nice things. Nowadays, those "nice things" come in the form of pottering around the farm, tinkering in the shed with the girls and visiting my brother-in-law's farm out west, which calms my mind a bit too.

'There're certainly things that I miss that maybe in time I'll get back to doing. I used to play golf each week with some mates, but for whatever reason we don't play anymore and I certainly wouldn't put myself through the thought of playing with people I don't know. I also really miss deep-sea fishing. I used to go with my brother and old man a bit and always enjoyed it. I've never really got seasick but these days, it's just an uneasy feeling I get with the swell.

'I've also learned not to expect a lot from other people in regards to support. The main reason is that not many people truly understand our lived experience. How could they? Unless of course they've actually lived through trauma of this nature. And even then, everyone's experience is different. This has also made me less judgemental of people who do things a little differently than most. If someone does something a bit weird or has an outside-the-box attitude towards something, the first thing I consider is that quite often, I haven't been in that situation, so I can't really pass judgement. I have most certainly done some weird shit myself!

'Throughout Ains' life, the thought of religion definitely stuck with me. I grew up Catholic and went to church every week with my old man. He used to tell us to thank God for all the good things you have in life and don't ask for anything extra. I did exactly that every week … apart from asking for the odd win at footy. I did all of it, in the hope that I'd get looked after a little bit in life. When Archie died, I still believed that maybe there was some sort of hope for me. But when Ains got crook, I was left to ponder why I even bothered. Sometimes, my mind would start racing and I would think things like, "If heaven is so good and two of my kids are there, why am I not there with them?" I felt a desire to be there with them … what I wouldn't give to be there with them. Nowadays, religion has somewhat lost me but, ironically, I still think my kids are in heaven … my heaven. I think everyone has their own version of heaven and it can be whatever they want it to be. I think I had a good childhood growing up as a Catholic and hence why my kids go to a Catholic school. I'll let them make up their own mind as to what they believe as they get older.

'There are so many moments in life that remind me of Archie and Ainsley. Everyday moments. I see kids their age and wonder what Archie and Ains would be like nowadays and it makes me realise all the things they've been robbed of, Ains in particular.'

Somewhere beyond right and wrong, there is a garden.
I will meet you there.

Rumi, 1207–73

EPILOGUE

That place

THE ACCLAIMED AUSTRALIAN singer Nick Cave knows about grief. He has lost two sons, and one of his albums, *Ghosteen*, was written in the wake of 15-year-old Arthur's sudden death. In an interview with ABC Radio's Richard Fidler, Cave was asked whether the grief alienated him from people, or brought him closer.

Cave said it brought him very close to people, eventually. First, he was obliterated by it with such force that it took some time to put himself back together 'in some way'.

'It's like you've been turned inside out … All the kind of self-regard I had – of my work and all the narcissism of my life – was put in the grinder and I just became a different person. Afterwards, I just was turned around to look at the world.'

Cave acknowledged that it took him a long time, and many tiny gestures from the world, to gently lead him there. In the beginning, nothing offered relief from his devastated state, not even for the shortest, fleeting moment.

'Initially … there was nothing good about it and there was nothing positive that I could say about it,' he said. 'In that place, there is no happy ending. Or it certainly feels that way.'

Aaron de Jong knows that place. Knows it all too well, in fact.

It's not simply being enclosed in a cave of rage, so to speak. Nor struggling at the bottom of a hole of devastation, a well of despair, waiting for a voice and a rope or a ladder to help you out. It's another existence, entirely, a universe of inexplicable loss, a world of torn human fabric, a place where the search for answers is endless and angst about the failures of society's systems eats away.

'Before, I was confident,' Aaron says. 'I was as confident as anything – probably a flog half the time. I wasn't just confident to take on anything. I'd take it on and I was going to win. Now? Nothing. I have none of that. Fuckin' nothing.'

Somehow, eventually, against the unfairness – that Great Unfairness of It All – courage weighs in. And courage measures up.

~

In the middle of 2017, Amanda de Jong enrolled in a nursing course at TAFE in Wagga Wagga. The idea came from Aaron after Amanda arrived home from a shift at the Coles supermarket, distraught, again, about a strange and ongoing occurrence.

'I was upset and angry as I had had an altercation with the mother of the girl that had pushed Ainsley,' she says. 'It wasn't the first time I had seen her at work. She came in numerous times, with or without her daughter, and on occasions with her husband. She was aware I worked there and would be laughing as she went about her shopping. Personally, I felt it was for me to know she was there.

'On this day I had confronted her and asked her: "Why? Why do you come to my workplace when there are so many other supermarkets you could do your shopping at? You bring your daughter here – how can you? Are you not normal?"

'When I arrived home that day, I said to Aaron, "That's it. I can't do this anymore." I used to be able to go about my job there in my own little bubble. It was where I could forget my nightmare for just a little bit. I also knew I had to keep working. I had two little girls and a husband to look after. In the months that followed Ainsley's passing, I wasn't sure if Aaron would be able to go back to work. To be honest, I wasn't sure if he would even be here …

'Anyway, in the days and weeks after I had that altercation, Aaron told me he had heard of the Assistant in Nursing course at TAFE. I had always admired the nurses for the work they did, especially throughout our journey with Ainsley. I remember thinking I would love to be a nurse; how cool would it be to help people? The nurses would make Ainsley laugh and they would dance with her, especially on her down days. They would treat her like a princess. They were Ainsley's little light and mine too. I was hesitant about the course as I hadn't been the most academic student at school and thought it would be way too hard. But I needed the change. I needed a challenge and I thought maybe – given what I had gone through with Ainsley – I might be able to relate to other mothers and parents and help in some small way.

'I will always be so appreciative and grateful for Aaron's encouragement for me to go ahead with the course, and for his support during it. It was a challenging time for us both. We were still trying to keep our heads above water, not drown in grief and anger, and trying to give Addison and Audrey a somewhat normal routine and life.

'When the course finished in late 2018, I was lucky enough to be offered a position at Wagga Base Hospital. The job was in the Emergency Department, where I had watched my little girl leave us. The fear and excitement was overwhelming. The thought that I would be working in the same environment where I had had to say goodbye to Ainsley scared me.

'Thankfully the hospital had undergone major construction and the ED looked totally different. I still had flashbacks on some occasions and spent a lot of quiet time in the change rooms pulling myself together. But remembering my girl always got me up and straight back to work. I ended up working alongside some of the nurses and doctors who fought so hard to keep our girl alive that day. The comfort and support they all gave me whilst I was in ED working, I will always be truly grateful for. Especially the nurse in charge, Bec ... who stood beside Aaron and me and did not leave us on the day we lost Ainsley. Who would have imagined I would be working alongside her.

'Coincidentally, Addison started school with Bec's son the following year. Bec was a big part of my nursing journey and still to this day is a very dear friend. I can honestly say nursing changed my life. It is rewarding but it's also challenging, mentally and emotionally. I walk past the morgue every morning and afternoon at work and still to this day my heart skips a beat. But, weirdly, I also feel close to Ains there.'

~

As Amanda studied and then embarked on her new career and a bold new chapter in life, Aaron kept up the struggle for answers, demanding accountability and examination. His courage well-and-truly measured up, too. Firstly, in the commitment and conviction to never waiver in his campaign to give Ainsley a voice; in his refusal to allow his daughter to be forgotten in society's maze of systems and processes. And secondly, when he allowed the search to turn in on himself.

Aaron began writing down his thoughts and memories of the years of Ainsley's life, and the troubled years that followed. In time, he mentioned it to a close friend, Ryan Forsyth, a former football teammate and a primary school teacher with an interest in writing. It proved a pivotal moment for Aaron, in coming to terms with Ainsley's life and death, and in restoring the value of friendships.

'When I started writing, I was in a really bad head space. I was angry and hating the world, wanting to start a fight about anything,' he says. 'At first, I would just write a few sentences on my phone as I was thinking about it. It didn't really make much sense. I had no intentions of anyone reading it – maybe just that one day someone might come across it and it might make sense to people as to why I am the way I am now.

'One night, "Forey" rang to see how I was going, as he often did. I knew he was educated in this type of thing, I knew he would be respectful and I trusted he would not tell anyone. And I knew he had the personality that could get this story going if I wanted to. I was pretty drunk this night though and I just blurted it out.'

Aaron hadn't even told Amanda that he had started writing down all that he could remember and how it had made him feel. Ryan, though, recognised the moment. The following day, he called and encouraged Aaron to follow through on his hunch and send all the notes he'd made. Ryan began working it into a document and, over time, Aaron's first account of 'Ainsley's Story' was written thanks to his good mate's encouragement, persistence and effort.

'It felt like a big relief when I told him. I didn't realise how much I had written down until I read back what he had put into a document. It took me a long time to read it as my emotions were everywhere,' Aaron says.

That was in 2021 and proved to be a significant step in a long journey aimed at restoring some emotional stability. The writing is raw and the act of opening up, courageous. Amanda was blown away by her husband's written account of memory and feeling, and his efforts to recognise their daughter's remarkable life, the horror of her death and its sickening aftermath.

Amanda followed suit, exploring her thoughts and recollections of the most difficult of times.

Some two years on, Aaron is still most comfortable at home with his girls, or sitting solo by a fire, staring into the flames in silent contemplation. His old self has vanished, like wisps of smoke climbing into the night sky. But he recognises he is improving, little bit by little bit, in terms of his ability to manage daily life and live with the pain of loss.

'If someone talks about Ains today, I still get that immediate emotional feeling in my chest,' he says. 'But it actually makes me feel happy for a while. I don't know if it's because someone else is thinking about her or just talking about her. Most of the thoughts I have of Ains now are the things that made me feel really proud back then, mostly how she kept proving everyone wrong with how her prognosis would go.

'I think I still push Addi and Aud maybe harder than I would have if we still had Ains. Having a child robbed of every opportunity, I have a bit of a "make the most of your opportunities and don't complain" attitude with them. The sadness, guilt and grief hasn't lightened at all for me. Guilt about work is one of the main feelings I have.

'I do feel, though, that I am an experienced griever, meaning, while it still hurts the same, I can hide it better and remove myself from situations I know will rattle me.'

What matters most to Ainsley's parents though is not their own state of being. It's fulfilling the mission to give her a voice, to recognise her strong and extraordinary spirit, and to offer their daughter the dignity her beautiful life demanded.

'Reading the book still gets me emotional. But I'm that bloody excited now it's about to be published,' Aaron says.

AUTOPSY REPORT

NEWCASTLE DEPARTMENT OF FORENSIC MEDICINE
NORTHERN FORENSIC HUB

EXTERNAL EXAMINATION PAEDIATRIC AUTOPSY REPORT FOR THE CORONER

Name: Ainsley Margaret DE JONG

Post mortem no: 141299

Age: 7 years (d.o.b. 07.12.06)

Sex: Female

Identification process:

Identified by: Wristband
Identified to: Dr A D Cala
Identified as: Ainsley De Jong

Pathologist: Dr Allan David CALA
M.B., BS, Dip RACOG, FRCPA
Senior Staff Specialist in Forensic Pathology

Time & date of autopsy: 9am on 21st October 2014

Place of autopsy: Newcastle Department of Forensic Medicine

Autopsy Assistant: David HODGSON

Police present at autopsy: Alex GILL, Newcastle Crime Scene

OPINION

I acknowledge that I have read the Expert Witness Code of Conduct in Schedule 7 of the NSW Uniform Civil Procedure Rules 2005; and agree to be bound by the code

Based on what I have observed, my experience and training, and the information supplied to me:

Ainsley Margaret De Jong died on 17th October 2014 at Wagga Base Hospital and that the cause of death is as follows:

1. DIRECT CAUSE:
   Disease or condition leading to death:

   (a) BLUNT FORCE HEAD INJURY IN A CHILD WITH PILOCYTIC ASTROCYTOMA

   ANTECEDENT CAUSES:
   Morbid conditions, if any, giving rise to the above cause, stating the underlying condition last:

   (b) ******

   (c) ******

2. Other significant conditions contributing to the death but not relating to the disease or condition causing it:

CIRCUMSTANCES OF DEATH:

The information provided at the time of autopsy was taken from the police form P79a.

This 7 year old girl had been diagnosed with a pilocytic astrocytoma (a malignant brain tumour especially affecting children) at age 4 months. The tumour was known to have been based around the pituitary fossa at the base of the brain and was known to have spread throughout the nervous system with spinal metastases present.

She had undergone surgery followed by chemotherapy and radiation therapy at Sydney Children's Hospital, Randwick, and was under the care of an oncologist in Sydney. She last underwent chemotherapy treatment two weeks prior to her death. She had severe visual impairment and moderate intellectual disability.

At the time of her death, she was attending Willans Hill School in Wagga Wagga. This is [a] school which caters for children with intellectual and other disabilities. She had been residing with her parents and siblings in the family home at Wagga.

During the lunch break on 17.10.14, Ainsley was in the playground and had been picking flowers. Another child pushed her to the upper chest region, causing her to fall backwards. The back of Ainsley's head struck a concrete surface. A teacher who had been present immediately went to her aid but by then, Ainsley was not moving.

Other staff were notified and Ainsley was attended to. At this time, Ainsley was unconscious and 'gulping' for air. An ambulance was called for, as was the child's father.

By the time [the] ambulance arrived, Ainsley's condition had deteriorated and she was pulseless. CPR was commenced and she was conveyed to Wagga Base Hospital. She was immediately attended to by doctors and was intubated. She had a cardiac arrest and was unable to be revived, with life pronounced extinct at 3.50pm.

A brain CT scan was able to be performed as part of resuscitation at the hospital. This showed the large pre-existent tumour with shunt *in situ*. Scalp bleeding was present at the back of the head and there was acute subdural bleeding.

COMMENTS:

1. An external examination in the presence of Crime Scene police and brain CT scan were performed.
2. An irregularly shaped area of abrasion was in the upper left parieto-occipital region near the vertex of the scalp (top of head), under which was scalp bruising.
3. There was fresh bleeding around the brain on CT scan. The base of the brain was abnormal with a large tumour evident in the region of the hypothalamus.

4. It seems likely the child sustained severe head impact trauma when she landed on a hard concreted surface. This appears to have caused a sudden but severe 'jolt' to the brain resulting in almost immediate loss of consciousness and cardiac arrest soon after.

5. Discussions were held with family members and coroners from Wagga and Sydney. Ultimately it was decided that a post mortem CT brain scan and external examination of the body were to be performed, and any further (invasive) procedure was not indicated under the circumstances.

DOCUMENTATION AND OTHER MATERIAL AVAILABLE:

At the time of the autopsy, the following documentation and material relating to the case has been made available to me:

1. Police Form P79A – Report of Death to the Coroner
2. Coroners Form 18 – Post Mortem Investigation Direction

SPECIMENS RETAINED FOR FURTHER EXAMINATION AND OTHER INVESTIGATION

Blood for storage.
Guthrie card.
Photography taken by Dr A D Cala and Alex Gill during the examination.
Braint CT scan

AUTOPSY FINDINGS

CLOTHING: The child was wearing a disposable nappy only.

EXTERNAL EXAMINATION:

The body was that of a well-nourished female that weighed 22 kilograms and measured 110cm length.
The scalp hair was brown and 20cm length.
The face was broadened as was the forehead.
There was slight 'bossing' of the forehead.
The neck appeared normal.
The eyebrows and eyelids were normal.

The eyes, sclera and conjunctivae were normal.
The irides were brown.
The cornea were translucent.
The nose was normal. The nostrils were clear.
The ears were normal in shape and size and the meati were normal.
The lips, gums and frenulum were normal.
The teeth were normally erupted for age, and were normal although two upper left incisor teeth were absent.
The chest, abdomen and back were normal.
The genitalia were those of a normal infant female.
The upper and lower extremities bilaterally were well developed and symmetrical.
The digits were normally developed and nails and creases were unremarkable.
The skin was normal with no evidence of jaundice, tumour or rash.
There was normal skin turgor.

POST MORTEM CHANGES:

The body was cold to touch.
Hypostasis was red and distributed posteriorly except in areas exposed to pressure.
Rigor mortis was wearing off
Decomposition changes were not present

MARKS or SCARS:

1. A curved 150mm right sided craniotomy scar.

2. A curved 80mm right occipital craniotomy scar.

3. 60mm scars below each breast.

EVIDENCE OF MEDICAL INTERVENTION:

1. An endotracheal tube exited the mouth.

2. An intravenous cannula in the right antecubital fossa

3. An intravenous cannula in the left antecubital fossa

EVIDENCE OF INJURY:

1. In the left upper parieto-occipital region of the head below the vertex was a collection of fine linear abrasions in an area 50mm diameter.
2. In the right upper forehead were three faint purple-red bruises in an area 25 × 15mm.
3. On the left shoulder was an area of yellowed abrasion 40mm diameter.

INTERNAL EXAMINATION

Not performed.

IMAGING:

Brain CT scan

Dr Allan David CALA
M.B., BS, Dip RACOG, FRCPA
Senior Staff Specialist in Forensic Pathology

8 December 2014